This book is for anyone who wants to understand what being more inclusive at work means, especially as it relates to black leaders. It is intended for those people who are saying "I don't know where to start," "I don't know what to do" and "I don't know what to say" when understanding and talking about race at work. Based on candid interviews with 30 successful black leaders, it peels away the multifaceted layers of black British leaders in organisations to offer a new way of thinking about the black British experience.

This book provides the insights and ideas required to have positive conversations about race at work and to create work environments where black leaders can thrive. In identifying the attributes and behaviours that successful black leaders have in common, this book offers new ways of thinking about black people at work that help to further inclusion. It shines a light on the daily reality of being a black leader in the workplace, providing an alternative entry point for conversations around inclusion and explores what individuals and organisations can do to increase inclusion in the workplace. Through first-hand stories this book explores the challenges, compromises, struggles and successes that black people encounter, and the range of strategies they employ to achieve success as they navigate the "white" workplace.

It is essential reading for business leaders in the private, public and third sector, human resources professionals, students, anyone teaching or mentoring black students or leaders and everyone interested in understanding race and furthering inclusion in the workplace.

Barbara Banda is the founder of the leadership consultancy, BarbaraBandaConsulting, which works with Fortune 500 and FTSE 100 companies. As Professor of Practice and Educator in Leadership, Inclusive Leadership, Strategy and Change at Duke Corporate Education, Rotterdam School of Management and Hult Ashridge, she is passionate about connecting leadership education to the realities of daily life in organisations. Barbara holds five degrees, including a D.Phil from the University of Oxford that explored the importance of connecting management education to the workplace, which informs her approach with clients. She is black British of Jamaican heritage.

"Barbara provides the insights leaders need to have an open and honest dialogue around self-disclosure and what being black – and more importantly a black leader – in the workplace means. It is a must read for both black and white leaders responsible for managing, skilling, reskilling, and hiring talent to improve culture and create a true merit-based workplace."

Rebecca Henderson,
*CEO Global Businesses and
Executive Board Member, Randstad*

"This book makes great strides in helping decision-makers think again about the nuances of diversity, equity and inclusion in organisations. It contains practical ideas that provide a springboard for a better understanding of the diverse communities on which global organisations rely for their success."

Jacky Wright,
Chief Digital Officer, Microsoft

"*The Model Black: How Black Leaders Succeed in Organisations and Why It Matters* gives a confronting and valuable insight into the experiences of black leaders in modern businesses. It gives a new, enriching perspective on how we can further diversity in companies by keeping an open mind regarding our mindset and attitude towards racial differences. This book therefore offers an accessible framework for rethinking the recruitment, retention and development of a diverse and cosmopolitan workforce."

Hans Sijbesma,
Country President at AstraZeneca

"Through engaging and authentic storytelling surrounding the British black experience, *The Model Black* unearths a still underrepresented factor critical to 21st Century leadership: the ability to navigate race productively but unapologetically. This book offers practical frameworks for managing this complex task for both black and non-black-ally leaders. The result is a compelling, accessible, and uplifting guide to confronting one of the most pressing needs of our age: rehumanizing our organizations."

Michael Chavez,
Global Managing Director,
Duke Corporate Education and co-author of
Rehumanizing Leadership:
Putting Purpose Back into Business

"Barbara has brilliantly articulated the real challenges that black professionals face in the British workforce every day. This book provides welcome relief and useful coping mechanisms for black leaders alongside new, invaluable insight for white leaders. There is a pragmatism and an optimism about this book that make it an engaging read with the clear purpose of moving us forward as professionals and also as a society. A must-read for leaders serious about creating a diverse and inclusive workplace."

Bridget Lea,
Managing Director of Commercial, BT

"This book possesses an honesty and a nuanced approach to the subject matter that is refreshing. Barbara has used the lived experiences of her interviewees to develop helpful frameworks. The entire book has an authentic tone that supports its practical call to action. This is a great piece of research that invoked frustration, concern and a desire to bring about change."

Naomi Dixon,
CEO Jewish Women's Aid

"Barbara refuses to tip-toe around one of the most important conversations of our time – race at work. She cuts to the chase with a deeply researched, practical guide that will transform all of us courageous enough to meaningfully explore our differences."

Desray Shuck,
Head of Technical Learning, Anglo American

THE MODEL BLACK

HOW BLACK BRITISH LEADERS SUCCEED IN ORGANISATIONS AND WHY IT MATTERS

Barbara Banda

Routledge
Taylor & Francis Group

LONDON AND NEW YORK

Cover image: © Getty Images | RyanJLane

First published 2022
by Routledge
4 Park Square, Milton Park, Abingdon, Oxon OX14 4RN

and by Routledge
605 Third Avenue, New York, NY 10158

Routledge is an imprint of the Taylor & Francis Group, an informa business

© 2022 Barbara Banda

British Library Cataloguing-in-Publication Data
A catalogue record for this book is available from the British Library

Library of Congress Cataloging-in-Publication Data
A catalog record for this book has been requested

ISBN: 978-1-032-06053-8 (hbk)
ISBN: 978-1-032-06054-5 (pbk)
ISBN: 978-1-003-20048-2 (ebk)

DOI: 10.4324/9781003200482

Typeset in Bembo

by Apex CoVantage, LLC

The Model Black, SCAN, The DARD Model and SQ are all Trade Marks

To Mummy, Daddy, John, Tasila, Thandiwe and Maiwa

CONTENTS

ACKNOWLEDGEMENTS

I would like to thank all the leaders who were part of the research that underpins this book. I am truly grateful that you all felt able to entrust me with your very personal stories and I hope that I have been able to communicate them in a way that has done them justice.

I would also like to thank my sisters Avella, Debbie and Carolyn for their contributions and patience and to my friends Anj, Ayiesha, Bob, Anne, Anna, Lorna, Jeremy and Liz for taking the time to offer me feedback on my drafts. Thanks also to my editor Kirsten for her insightful ideas and encouragement.

I am grateful to my daughter Tasila for her immeasurable patience as a sparring partner and sounding board, helping me to synthesise my thoughts and to develop and refine many of the concepts. A particular thank-you to my daughter Maiwa for providing a constant supply of tea and for fuelling my mind with the most delicious home-made cooking! Also to my daughter Thandiwe for her wisdom and good humour and for keeping me calm and balanced throughout. And to my husband, John, for giving me the space to complete this project.

A very special thanks to my brother, Robert, who held my hand and offered me unwavering support on this entire book journey.

ABOUT THE AUTHOR

Barbara Banda is the founder of the leadership consultancy, Barbara-BandaConsulting, which works with Fortune 500 and FTSE 100 companies. As Professor of Practice and Educator in leadership, Inclusive Leadership, Strategy and change at Duke Corporate Education, Rotterdam School of Management and Hult Ashridge, she is passionate about connecting leadership education to the realities of daily life in organisations. Prior to her business school career, Barbara held senior positions in marketing and strategy in global organisations. Barbara holds five degrees, including a D.Phil from the University of Oxford that explored the importance of connecting management education to the workplace, which informs her approach with clients. She is black British of Jamaican heritage.

ABBREVIATIONS

CBE   Commander of the Order of the British Empire
FTSE   Financial Times Share Index
GCSE   General Certificate in Secondary Education
OBE   Officer of the Order of the British Empire

INTRODUCTION

"As a black woman, I see things rather differently."
"I don't see you as black."
"Why not? I <u>am</u> black."
"I've never seen you as black."
"I've always been black."

OWNING MY IDENTITY AS A BLACK BRITISH LEADER

It was the first time I had ever mentioned my colour in conversation with Tony.

It was also the first time I had referred to myself as "black" in his presence.

I had known Tony, a long-standing white friend and colleague, for years and never contemplated making any comment about my skin colour. I was concerned that any mention of my skin colour might make him feel uncomfortable and affect our relationship or my future work prospects. I also knew that comments around colour might make me seem like one of *those* blacks – one of *those* blacks you have to watch what you say around, *those* blacks who played the "race card," *those* blacks who Tony could not conveniently relate to in the way he could to the white people he knew. However, I wished that instead of denying or dancing around my difference, my colleague Tony had felt able to talk about it with me. I wished he had the vocabulary and the confidence to discuss what being black in the workplace meant to me. He might have begun to understand how much of myself I felt unable to bring to work.

DOI: 10.4324/9781003200482-1

This "self-disclosure" represented a pivotal moment in our relationship. It was also a turning point for me. I began acknowledging my colour and my difference to white people in a way that I had never done before. I was talking about a part of me that had always been there, but it was a part that I had chosen not to speak about to my white colleagues. I was in my mid-50s, a relatively successful black woman with five degrees, including an Oxford doctorate . . . yet I felt uncomfortable about fully owning my blackness among white colleagues. Not any kind of white people; these were typically people I felt could impact my ability to earn a living.

I learnt very early in my career that referring to my race at work was dangerous for career progression. I once corrected my white manager on his inappropriate language use and was thereafter referred to by the team as "PC (politically correct) Banda." The situation escalated, and their boss, a well-meaning director, warned me, "Barbara, if you keep saying things like that, no one on the team will want to work with you." Recognising that commenting on issues of race at work was met by mockery, defensiveness or pity meant that it was so much easier not to talk about it. I could be black as long as I adopted the kind of black identity that white people felt comfortable around.

Life became much easier for my colleagues and me when I behaved like one of those blacks who were "easy to work with," did not call out unsavoury comments and, consequently, did not negatively affect the working atmosphere. So, despite countless other occasions when I could have taken offence, I eased on through most of my career as the smiling black lady who never seemed bothered.

By 2017, I was getting tired of being that woman. I quit my full-time position as a professor of practice to work for myself and discovered the delights of very occasionally talking about being black. I noticed a distinct change in the atmosphere when I did it with people who had known me for a long time – not necessarily unpleasant, just different. Nevertheless, there was a refreshing sense of being more myself when I raised it with a new contact. I knew I needed to be extremely cautious and very selective. I still wanted to earn a living. I was much more attractive to clients as the black lady who was not *too* black than as the black lady who might be one of *those* blacks.

The murder of George Floyd in 2020 triggered a global outpouring of grief, anger and a sense of injustice. Black people everywhere told their stories about being black amid a tsunami of interviews, reports and articles. Many of us with longer memories feared for those black British workers who were telling their stories; we hoped they were not foolish enough to be *too* honest. In the wrong organisations and contexts, too much "self-disclosure" would surely backfire once the media energy had moved on to the next newsworthy topic.

Once my process of "self-disclosure" was underway amongst my colleagues, there was no going back. I have noticed an impact on those relationships that were previously safe. I spoke about my black experience with a colleague who now frames much of her conversation with me as "we white people." It sounds a bit strange. Maybe it sounded odd to her when I referred to my being a "black person?" But she is trying to navigate her new understanding of who she now thinks I am – though I keep reminding her that I am the same person I always was. I simply want to share more of who I am with her.

Reflecting on my career, I realise that I have been managing my career as a "black professional." What I mean by that is that I had, consciously or subconsciously, chosen not to foreground my race. This strategy enabled me to successfully navigate my workplaces as a black woman. It kept me safe and white people comfortable. My brother, Professor Robert Beckford, took a different route. Robert has lived his entire career as a "professional black," foregrounding his race and vociferously advocating for black British people. The research for this book indicates that successfully navigating public- and private-sector organisations in Britain almost always requires black people to behave as "black professionals." Further, most black leaders agree that the moment a black leader can become less "black professional" and more of a "professional black" is either after you have become successful enough to speak out or at the point when you no longer have skin in the game in the organisation.

The Model Black: How Black British Leaders Succeed in Organisations and Why It Matters represents the beginning of my transition out of being a fully fledged "black professional." Does this public "self-disclosure" make me a "professional black?" Or is there a middle ground? This "self-disclosure" means three things are certain. First, doing it feels good! It feels as though a burden has been lifted. There is a sense of freedom that comes with leaning into all of who you are. Second, there is a real prospect of being judged and misunderstood. Third, making this shift in such a public way means there is no going back. Once you have talked publicly about your race, you cannot pretend that you have not done it. There is no going back. This may result in certain doors no longer being open to me. There may be new and more exciting doors, but some will have closed irrevocably – and I may never know what they are.

In writing this book, I thought hard about whether my "self-disclosure" and the disclosures by black leaders were necessary. Were we revealing stories that could be used to punish, diminish or even manipulate us in the workplace? However, like bell hooks,[1] I feel that this openness has the power to heal and to make new growth possible. These revelations have all been put forward in the service of fostering greater understanding and advancing inclusion.

WHY I WROTE THIS BOOK

For over 20 years, I have trained senior leaders in leadership, strategy and change as part of large, often complex global leadership development initiatives. I became a professor of practice at a global business school. As part of this work, I have been privileged to travel to wonderful locations, indulge in delicious food and connect with the most talented people. These individuals are well-educated, highly motivated and, by and large, wonderful human beings.

Interacting with leaders has taught me so much about business, leadership and organisational culture. These leaders have shown dignity, strength, courage, openness, vulnerability and humility as they seek to better themselves and their organisations. They have a deep desire to improve the culture of their organisations through gaining a better understanding of themselves and changing their behaviour.

What is always noticeable to me as a black woman is that I rarely meet people who look like me; of the many thousands of managers across a wide range of organisations and cultures I have worked with, I have encountered very few black leaders. Even fewer of them are black *and* British. It has never bothered me; most of the groups I work with are predominantly white, and I am black. We still make deep connections, and I always endeavour to do my very best to help them develop further as leaders. This is the work I love,

and I wish the same joy in their work for all participants that I inter-
act with!

There is, however, one blind spot to these interactions: in these
mainly white rooms, I have noticed that the few black leaders I meet
often request to "speak privately" with me. Black leaders value the
opportunity to share one-to-one what it is *really* like for them in
their organisations with someone they feel understands their daily
challenges. Often, they want me to know that although they have
been selected for a prestigious leadership development programme,
it does not mean that they are not struggling with the daily weight
of being visually different in their organisations. They wanted to
reveal what they were doing to succeed – they just did not want to
do so publicly. This book seeks to share experiences like theirs.

*The Model Black: How Black British Leaders Succeed in Organisations
and Why It Matters* contains honest stories based on interviews with
30 successful black British leaders. These are, in the main, leaders
outside of the limelight; like me, they have "got on" with doing a
good job, finding ways of navigating British workplaces as a black
person in organisations where most of the people at their level do
not look like them. These leaders do not view themselves as victims.
They are surviving and thriving.

In this book, black leaders share their voices and their challenges,
the sacrifices and successes they have experienced as they have
sought to navigate a white world. By navigate, I mean find their way
through to the middle or top of the organisation. Their agreement
to be honest and open is in service of their black and white colleagues, and with the intention that we can all become more comfortable talking about the issue of race at work and, in so doing,
create true merit-based workplaces. Some of the leaders have chosen
to be named in the book. Others wanted to be anonymised. In both
cases, their shared hope is that by publishing their real stories, they
will support organisations to become more inclusive to people who
look like them; people of black African, black Caribbean and mixed-
race heritage. It is important that, amid all the noise around race and
Black Lives Matter, these often-silent individuals are heard. These
leaders' stories offer insights into the black experience that might
help move the inclusivity dial by even a tiny amount.

The aim of this book is to offer new ways of thinking about black
people at work that help us all have different conversations. It seeks

to offer a new paradigm for understanding the black British experience. It is the book I would have liked my colleague Tony to have read. It represents my contribution towards creating more inclusive workplaces, spaces where black leaders can perform at their best. My intention is to shine a light on the experiences of black people in a way that contributes to a positive conversation about race at work. I am mindful of my daughters' words – my middle girl pleads, "Mummy, please don't write another book about how awful it is to be black, we have enough of those!" and my eldest, who insists that this book be "suitably layered in a way that discusses the complexities and multifaceted nature of being black in a British workplace."

To this end, I am delighted to introduce you to the stories and perspectives of the black leaders in organisations across Britain. Together we will peel back the layers and share the complex realities and how we successfully navigate our organisations.

My hope is that as you read this book, you are able to suspend judgement and put aside any preconceptions you may have of what life might be like for black leaders in organisations. I invite you to be curious about their experiences and reflect on what we might all learn from them.

WRITTEN FOR WHITE READERS, EMBRACED BY BLACK LEADERS

In the post-George Floyd era, many people want a better understanding of the black British experience. They want to know how they can support the broader cause of greater inclusivity in the workplace and in life more generally. This book is essential reading for business leaders in the private, public and third sector, human resources (HR) professionals, students and anyone teaching or mentoring black students or leaders. Indeed, it is essential reading for anyone interested in understanding race and promoting inclusion. This book is intended for white leaders who are saying – "I don't know where to start," "I don't know what to do" and "I don't know what to say" when understanding and talking about race at work. It is of broader interest to those interested in debates about identity and representation and how these relate to work.

I set out to write this book for white readers, to offer them a new perspective on the black leadership experience. I hope I have succeeded in this. However, the more I shared the content of the book, the more it became clear how much there is in it for black leaders. They found it liberating to learn the language to understand, articulate and frame their daily experiences. So, I offer them the language of the "Model Black" to express the multifaceted layers of black leadership.

Whilst this book is about the black experience, it will also resonate with those seeking to understand the organisational experience of other under-represented groups, such as women and those from the LGBTQ+ community, and how they can best support them.

PLEASE CALL ME "BLACK"

In the weeks leading up to writing this book, a company invited me to coach a black leader. When the white HR executive shared the leader's name, I suggested they were of Caribbean descent. The executive looked bemused.

"Actually, I have no idea," she responded. "Maybe. Or African."

I realised the importance of a deeper understanding of some of the nuances of what it means to be black in Britain. Black, Asian, and minority ethnic or BAME (said "b-ay-m") is a blanket term that does not allow for the distinction between cultures, ethnicities or countries of origin. I tend to agree with Sir Trevor Philips, OBE,[2] former head of the Commission for Racial Equality. He suggests that "BAME" and similar terms can be divisive and mask the disadvantages specific ethnic groups face. More recently, The controversial *Report of the Commission for Race and Ethnic Disparities*[3] also called for the term to be replaced. To conflate the perspectives and experiences of black Caribbeans with black Africans can be unhelpful. Even within a continent, grouping together, for example, Nigerians with South Africans can also be problematic.

All the black leaders I spoke to for this book considered themselves to be black, whether they were of Caribbean, African or mixed-race heritage. Black may seem all-encompassing. However, if we need a term, let's use black, but let us also recognise its complexities.

The term "black" has been associated with various connotations over the years. In the UK, "black" was historically used to refer to black people of African descent and, later, expanded to include people of Asian origin. By the end of the 1980s, "black" reverted to mean only those of African descent. "Black" became a political term adopted by those of African and Caribbean heritage because of its use in the black consciousness and civil rights movement. For those who identified with it, the term was embraced as a label of pride and beauty.

Consequently, being referred to as "black" is a source of pride. I like being called "black." It describes my skin colour, my heritage and my pride. However, being black describes only a part of who I am. I am black and a woman born and brought up in England. My parents are from Jamaica, and I describe myself as being of Jamaican or Caribbean heritage. I am also black British. I am married to a black man who describes himself as Zambian, not African. We have black children who share a black African and a black Caribbean heritage (a box that does not exist when selecting heritage on most forms – it is either black African or black Caribbean, not both) and refer to themselves as black British or mixed black African and Caribbean. Two of my sisters' partners identify as white and British, and some of their children like to be called "mixed race" or of "mixed heritage," and some of them prefer not to be labelled at all.

I cannot remember when I stopped being "coloured" and started being "black." I was the only coloured girl at school and university and became the only black woman at work. I was the only black graduate in the marketing departments of my first and second employers in the pharmaceutical industry. When I joined a global healthcare company in 1990, my new manager introduced me to the marketing director. Following a warm welcome, I left the room. My manager, who had stayed behind, chuckled playfully as she recounted the events after I had left the room.

"She's black!" the marketing director had exclaimed.

"Yes – I had noticed!"

I laughed too. "Black" is not a dirty word. It's part of who I am.

WE ARE NOT ALL BLACK OR WHITE

In this book, I have chosen to talk about black and white in essentialist terms. We know that individuals do not belong to only one or other of these categories. However, I have done this intentionally for the purposes of writing a critique. When I talk about "black," I am referring very specifically to black leaders who are African, African Caribbean or of mixed African or African Caribbean heritage.[4] There may be individuals who consider themselves brown, those of Asian or other origins who consider themselves physically or politically black. These groups are not included in my definition. I cannot and do not claim to write for everyone who considers themselves to be black. Indeed there will be thousands of individuals of African and African Caribbean descent who also believe that I am not speaking for them!

BLACK BRITISH LEADERS: PRIVATE, VARIED, YET SIMILAR

Books and articles on black British leadership tend to focus on the "most influential" or the "most powerful" black Britons. The spotlight is on black exceptionalism – black people who are seen as rich, powerful, authoritative or famous. There is real value in such articles as they can help to break down negative stereotypes around black Britons and provide much-needed role models. However, they do not focus on the thousands of successful black professionals working in organisations. Their stories mainly remain hidden. These regular workers do not proclaim to be black leaders. In many cases, these black professionals may have made an active choice not to claim leadership. To do so would mean dealing with the additional scrutiny of both being black and being in a leadership role. These black professionals may not perceive themselves as leaders as they go about succeeding in their professional roles. Equally, they may not feel they have experiences others want to hear about. This book is intended to tell their stories of successfully navigating white workspaces. These stories point to the need for meaningful change in the ways in which black people are perceived and treated in organisations if the organisations genuinely want black people to feel included.

Are black leaders different to white leaders? In the workplace, black leaders do exactly the same work as white leaders! Leaders lead people, processes and expert functions. They manage change in a competitive and volatile world. They set direction and align and motivate people to achieve the organisation's goals. Leading has been contrasted with managing, which is about staffing, budgeting, controlling and managing the here and now.[5] However, there is an intersection between the two. Leaders manage; managers lead. Like many leaders, therefore, the black leaders interviewed for this book have an eye on the day-to-day tasks whilst focussing on their people and the broader strategic issues. But, whilst black leaders strive to carry out the same role as white leaders, there are several significant differences.

When it comes to the work itself, black leaders are "doing" the same job as white leaders, with an additional separate and deeper layer. The leaders interviewed for this book revealed much about the choices related to their colour they make on a daily basis – choices regarding their behaviour, the way they approach their work and the way they express their identity. The primary reason for this is that black leaders are faced with stereotypes of black people that permeate society more generally. Consider the research from Duffy et al.[6] that one in eight Britons believed that black people have lower earnings because they lack motivation or willpower. Privately, propaganda and poorly written media remind people that "black men are threatening" and "black women are angry."

Many black leaders also feel that they cannot honestly tell their full leadership story, as they do not want to offend the institutions they rely on for their living. A friend recently appeared in an article about successful minorities. She is the most senior black person in a global engineering company. In the article, this black leader described her route to senior management and praised her organisation for its response to George Floyd's death and the subsequent Black Lives Matter protests. Privately, she told me how disappointed she was with the company's response. Successful black leaders are often expected to sanitise their stories for the benefit of their white audience and their future career prospects. This is not something that they complain about – it is an unwritten rule of becoming and remaining successful. So it was unsurprising that the published work included a mere fraction of my friend's real leadership story.

There is no uniform type of black British leader and thus no ubiquitous black British leadership experience. Every black leader has their own intersectionalities with class, gender and sexual orientation. Some are educated abroad, others in the UK. Each black leader has individual personality traits, unique ways of thinking and behaving. Black leaders may not like or even get along with each other. But is it possible that they share similarities in how they have navigated to the top? When I started this project, my knowledge was limited to my own experience and that of family and friends. This book reveals many more experiences, but only a small number of specific strategies that black leaders employ to navigate the workplace and succeed.

THE BUSINESS CASE FOR INCLUSION

There is a business case for inclusion and a moral case for inclusion. At face value, the business case would seem obvious; teams with a diversity of thought are likely to develop a broader range of ideas and solutions. Indeed, the rationale for a diverse workforce laid out by Konrad in 2003[7] still holds in organisations today. She argued that a more diverse workforce means that businesses that wish to attract and retain the best quality talent would have to recruit from all demographic categories. Secondly, a more diverse society together with a globalised marketplace and more diverse customer base means that businesses that employ a more diverse workforce will better be able to sell to a customer base made up of different cultural backgrounds. Thirdly, demographically diverse groups can outperform other groups in problem-solving and creativity tasks because they have a greater variety of information experience and perspectives.

At first glance, there is now an increasing body of data that demonstrates higher financial returns from diverse organisations. A 2018 Boston Consulting Group study[8] suggests that increasing the diversity of leadership teams leads to more and better innovation and improved financial performance, resulting in a 19 per cent increase in revenue. The study reported that in both developing and developed economies, those companies with above-average diversity on their leadership teams report a greater payoff from innovation and higher earnings before interest and taxes margins. Their data showed that companies could start generating gains with relatively small changes in the make-up of their teams. Similarly, a McKinsey report[9] established a correlation between significant levels of diversity in company leadership and a greater likelihood of outperforming the relevant industry peer group on profitability. The report also found that, with respect to ethnic and cultural diversity, more diverse companies were 33 per cent more likely to outperform their peers on profitability. *People Management* reported a study that analysed around 600 business decisions made by 200 teams.[10] It found that geographically diverse teams make better business decisions 87 per cent of the time. That study also identified that business decisions were better when there was gender diversity and increased further where there was geographic diversity.

Many companies have a diverse workforce, but they are not inclusive. As one leader told me, "Some workplaces like mine look representative, there is an abundance of colour, but that does not tell you about what the temperature feels like inside." We talk about diversity being about inviting people to the party, and inclusion is about asking them to dance. I would take this analogy further. Inclusion is about creating a space where everyone feels free to dance their authentic dance without being judged. It is about appreciating and being curious about other people's dancing styles, being open to changing your style of dancing to include aspects of theirs. In this way, the party gets better and better as the night goes on as everyone feels able to fully express themselves through their individual dance styles. Inclusion takes time. It requires time to develop relationships and safe spaces where everyone can truly be who they want to be at work.

The importance of leveraging diversity through inclusive practices is reinforced by Ely and Thomas;[11] they argue that rigorous, peer-reviewed studies found no significant relationships between board gender diversity or racial diversity and financial performance. The researchers also assert that diversity does contribute to higher-quality work, better decision-making, greater team satisfaction and more equality – under certain circumstances. Performance can be enhanced when team members are capable of reflecting on how they work together, the status differences among ethnic groups are minimised and team members are willing to learn from each other's differences. However, they suggest that this is unlikely to have a direct effect on the bottom line. They believe it is not enough to simply recruit for visual difference. It is important to tap into the identity-related knowledge and experiences that these groups possess. This may require changes to the corporate culture and power structure.

There is also the moral case for diversity and inclusion. Indeed, some suggest that the financial case is counterproductive. The business case does little to empower minority groups and can even be turned against such groups if becoming more diverse has a negative impact on performance. Instead, we need a moral case that is based on treating individuals equally. This is simply about us being good human beings.

Barbara Banda
barbara@bbcons.co.uk
London, April 2022

NOTES

1 hooks, b. (1989). *Talking Back: Thinking Feminist, Thinking Black* (Vol. 10). Boston, MA: South End Press.

2 Okolosie, L. et al. Is It Time to Ditch the Term 'Black Asian and Minority Ethnic' (BAME)? *The Guardian.* www.theguardian.com/commentis-free/2015/may/22/black-asian-minority-ethnic-bame-bme-trevor-phillips-racial-minorities [Last accessed November 2021].

3 Commission on Race and Ethnic Disparities. (2021). The Report of the Commission on Race and Ethnic Disparities. *The Guardian.*

4 This book does include one interview with an American working in Britain.

5 Mintzberg, H. (2013). *Simply Managing: What Managers Do – and Can Do Better.* San Francisco: Berrett-Koehler Publishers Inc.

6 Duffy, B., Hewlett, K., Hesketh, R., Benson, R., & Wager, A. (2021). *Unequal Britain: Attitudes to Inequalities After Covid-19.* The Policy Institute. Kings College London. https://doi.org/10.18742/pub01-043 [Last accessed 22 July 2021].

7 Konrad, A. M. (2003). Special Issue Introduction: Defining the Domain of Workplace Diversity Scholarship. *Group & Organization Management* 28(1), 4–17.

8 Lorenzo, R., et al. (2018, January 23). *How Diverse Leadership Teams Boost Innovation.* Boston: Boston Consulting Group; Hunt, V., Prince, S., Dixon-Fyle, S., & Yee, L. (2018). Delivering Through Diversity. *McKinsey & Company* 231.

9 Hunt, V., Prince, S., Dixon-Fyle, S., & Yee, L. (2018). Delivering Through Diversity. *McKinsey & Company* 231.

10 People Management Editorial. (2017). *Diversity Drives Better Decisions,* 23 October. www.peoplemanagement.co.uk/experts/research/diversity-drives-better-decisions [Last accessed 31 July 2021]; Larson, E. (2017). White Paper: Hacking Diversity with Inclusive Decision Making. *Cloverpop.* https://www.cloverpop.com/hubfs/Whitepapers/Cloverpop_Hacking_Diversity_Inclusive_Decision_Making_White_Paper.pdf [Last accessed February 2022].

11 Ely, R. J., & Thomas, D. A. (2020). Getting Serious About Diversity. *Harvard Business Review* 98(6), 114–122.

REFERENCES

Bell, E. L. J. E., & Nkomo, S. M. (2001). *Our Separate Ways: Black and White Women and the Struggle for Professional Identity*. Boston, MA: Harvard Business School Press.

Chobot-Mason, D., & Thomas, K. M. (2002). Minority Employees in Majority Organizations: The Interaction of Individual and Organizational Racial Identity in the Workplace. *Human Resource Development Review* 1, 323–344.

DiMillo, V., Brown, A., & Harrington, B. (2021). Addressing Race in the Workplace: Advancing Diversity, Equity, and Inclusion. *Boston College Center for Work & Family-Executive Briefing Series*.

Dixon-Fyle, S., Dolan, K., Hunt, V., & Prince, S. (2020). *Diversity Wins: How Inclusion Matters*. McKinsey & Company.

Duffy, B., Hewlett, K., Hesketh, R., Benson, R., & Wager, A. (2021). *Unequal Britain: Attitudes to Inequalities after Covid-19*. The Policy Institute. Kings College London. https://doi.org/10.18742/pub01-043 [Last accessed 22 July 2021].

Ely, R. J., & Thomas, D. A. (2020). Getting Serious About Diversity. *Harvard Business Review* 98(6), 114–122.

Gompers, P., & Kovvali, S. (2018). The Other Diversity Dividend. *Harvard Business Review*.

Green, J., & Hand, J. R. (2021). *Diversity Matters/Delivers/Wins Revisited in S&P 500® Firms*. SSRN 3849562. https://papers.ssrn.com/sol3/papers.cfm?abstract_id=3849562.

Hales, C. P. (2019). What do Managers do? A Critical Review of the Evidence. *Managerial Work* 263–290.

hooks, b. (1986). Talking Back. *Discourse* 123–128.

hooks, b. (1989). *Talking Back: Thinking Feminist, Thinking Black* (Vol. 10). Boston, MA: South End Press.

Hunt, V., Prince, S., Dixon-Fyle, S., & Yee, L. (2018). Delivering Through Diversity. *McKinsey & Company* 231.

Jayne, M. E., & Dipboye, R. L. (2004). Leveraging Diversity to Improve Business Performance: Research Findings and Recommendations for Organizations. *Human Resource Management: Published in Cooperation with the School of Business Administration, The University of Michigan and in alliance with the Society of Human Resources Management* 43(4), 409–424.

Jones, J. M. (2003). Constructing Race and Deconstructing Racism: A Cultural Psychology Approach. In G. Bernai, J. E. Trimble, A. K. Burlew, & F. T. L. Leong (Eds.), *Handbook of Racial and Ethnic Minority Psychology* (pp. 276–290). Thousand Oaks, CA: Sage.

Kanter, R. M. (1995). *The Change Masters: Corporate Entrepreneurs at Work*. London: Routledge.

Konrad, A. M. (2003). Special Issue Introduction: Defining the Domain of Workplace Diversity Scholarship. *Group & Organization Management* 28(1), 4–17.

Kotter, J. P. (1982, November–December). What Effective General Managers Really Do. *Harvard Business Review*.

Larson, E. (2017). *White Paper: Hacking Diversity with Inclusive Decision Making*. Cloverpop.

Lorenzo, R., et al. (2018, January 23). *How Diverse Leadership Teams Boost Innovation*. Boston Consulting Group.

Mintzberg, H. (2013). *Simply Managing: What Managers Do – and Can Do Better*. San Francisco: Berrett-Koehler Publishers Inc.

Minzberg, H. (1988). The Manager's Job: Folklore and Fact. In J. B. Quinn, R. M. James, & H. Mintzberg (Eds.), *The Strategy Process* (p. xxv, 998). Englewood Cliffs: Prentice-Hall International.

Okolosie, L., et al. Is it Time to Ditch the Term 'Black Asian and Minority Ethnic' (BAME)? *The Guardian*. www.theguardian.com/commentisfree/2015/may/22/black-asian-minority-ethnic-bame-bme-trevor-phillips-racial-minorities [Last accessed November 2021].

People Management Editorial. (2017, October 23). *Diversity Drives Better Decisions*. www.peoplemanagement.co.uk/experts/research/diversity-drives-better-decisions [Last accessed 31 July 2021].

Powerful Media. (2021). *Blackpowerlist*. www.powerful-media.co.uk/powerlist [Last accessed September 2021].

Smith, C. R. (2018). The Role of Self-Disclosure in Improving Workplace Cross-Race Mentoring Outcomes. *CUNY Academic Works*. https://academicworks.cuny.edu/gc_etds/2879

Stewart, R. (1988). *Managers and their Jobs: A Study of the Similarities and Differences in the Ways Managers Spend their Time*. Basingstoke: Macmillan.

HOW THIS BOOK IS STRUCTURED

This book is divided into three sections.

Section 1 provides an insight into the range of situations that black leaders learn to navigate and explains how they do it. It begins by discussing how black leaders learn to navigate race at work. It then sets out a new framework for understanding black leaders and explores how they navigate the educational system. It describes the daily incidents of racism and how successful black leaders respond.

Section 2 discusses how black leaders conduct themselves in order to succeed. It puts forward the concept of the Model Black as a new trope that describes the attributes and behaviours of successful black leaders.

Section 3 suggests how individuals and organisations can work with this new understanding of black leadership to advance diversity, equity, and inclusion in the workplace. In the final chapter, I speak with younger professionals and consider the future of the Model Black.

DOI: 10.4324/9781003200482-2

SECTION 1

HOW WE GOT HERE

1

"ANYWHERE EXCEPT THE MEAT COUNTER"

This chapter

- *discusses how black people learn, from their first employment, to navigate race at work;*
- *explains how black leaders use the SCAN model to deal with race "in the moment";*
- *explores the impact of a decade of reports on race in the workplace; and*
- *raises the challenge of talking about race at work – why do we still find it so difficult?*

Everybody's got a mother, or a father or brother or sister, and so on and so forth. I think the problem with race is that the other side of the line lies behind an opaque curtain. You literally don't know what's on the other side of that curtain – and by and large, how would you? Neither you nor I have ever been, by definition, in a circumstance where everybody in the room is white.

Sir Trevor Phillips, OBE, Writer,
Broadcaster and Former Head of the
Commission for Racial Equality

People aren't actively excluding *people*, not consciously necessarily, but the *behaviours* and what they *expect* of people, thus, by implication, they're excluding people. So, this exclusion occurs often by accident . . . the majority of [white] people that you'd

DOI: 10.4324/9781003200482-4

encounter that are professionals were actually good human beings who wanted to see people succeed.

Michael Sherman, Chief Transformation
and Strategy Officer, BT

You could just have a simple, zero-tolerance rule, that says, "Every time I experience racism of any type, I'm just going to go full-out and confront it." Or you could have another simple rule which is like a lot of recent immigrants have done over the years, which is, "I'm going to keep my head down, and ignore it all. I'm just part of it. Grin and bear it." There are two extreme rules. Neither of them, in my experience, work. In the middle, is me trying to figure out, on one day, I'm going to confront that . . . the way in which you respond – and this is the difficult part of the quiz show – the choices you make affect how people perceive you.

Paul Cleal, OBE, Former Partner, PwC

It seemed like in the UK, no one even talked about race. The only thing that people successfully talked about in the boardroom or the executive meetings would be gender. We actually had what I consider progressive discussion around gender and gender equality. Gender is easier: Even broaching the subject of race was taboo which was quite shocking because, in America, it's front and centre.

Anon, Senior Executive, Technology

Everyone sees colour. You may not act on what you see, but you do see colour. It's just like saying, "I don't see sexual orientation," or "I don't see gender." Those are all lies. Don't perpetuate those lies and tell those lies to your colleagues because it just makes the mantra that makes it harder for your diverse colleagues.

Anon, Senior Executive, Automotive

LEARNING TO NEED TO NAVIGATE RACE AT WORK

I got my first job in 1979. I was 16 and in need of a job to supplement my meagre income from pocket money. The previous month of Saturdays had been a steady routine of "get up – get dressed – head to the market" and then spend the next few hours asking stall-holders for work. I was prepared to begin work that very day, I would tell them. Every time I would get the same reaction: a brief glance but no work available.

I was delighted when I got a job in the branch of a national super-market chain. Forty years later, I still remember the interview: a lengthy one-way conversation with a personnel lady in a small but clean upstairs office. After rattling through the standard questions, the interviewer, satisfied with my answers, laid out the terms of employment – £12 for 11 hours of work per week. I vividly recall her smile; she wore it throughout the interview, from beginning to end. It was a just-warm-enough professional upward curve of the lips, painted with pink lipstick. She probably wore that smile even when she fired people.

Nothing was said about my race, apart from one thing.

"You'll be treated exactly like all the other Saturday Girls," the personnel lady said. "And you can do everything the white girls can – except work on the meat counter." I blinked. Her smile didn't move. "It puts the customers off," she said by way of explanation, totally matter of fact.

There was no tension, ill will or any kind of emotion between us. In the moment, I didn't think much of this information. Like many teenagers (both then and now), I was just happy to have a part-time job. No nonsense comment about meat counters was going to discourage me.

My interview took place at a point in history when male store managers still openly and overtly slapped the ladies' bottoms to speed up shelf stacking. So, when I shared what the personnel lady had said with my friends, both black and white, we all treated it as a joke. Without overthinking it, we laughed about the possible unpleasant connections between a black shop assistant and the meat counter. Would a cut or plaster on my finger make people think a piece of my finger had fallen into their meat? Did they think I was dirty? Or muddy?

I enjoyed my time as Saturday Girl. To me, aged 16, the role was sufficiently exciting and varied. I trained on the tills, finding immense satisfaction in being able to punch in numbers without looking at the keys, and I got real energy from talking to the customers who passed through, taking what felt like several minutes to write out their cheques. My customers were, on the whole, engaging and positive.

On one occasion, one of my teachers (a vicar, who taught religious education) came through my till with his shopping, chatting away. Noticing he had forgotten his jelly babies at the back of the till, he grabbed the packet, laughing gleefully.

"I enjoy biting the heads off the black ones," he grinned, adding them to his shopping. I thought it was a stupid comment. Again, though, I didn't feel any anger or emotion or anything that the 21st-century Barbara suggests I should have felt. At that stage of my life, I was accustomed to teachers and others in authority making ignorant and offensive comments about my race. That was part of my daily life. So, this was the behaviour of a stupid, ignorant man. I shrugged it off. My job was to work on the tills, not discuss black jelly babies.

Unconsciously, I was navigating race in the workplace at 16 years old. And without ever making a purposeful choice, I had developed a strategy for doing so: keep my head down, work hard and ignore any comments about colour.

On reflection, I can now view the time at the store from two different perspectives (Figure 1.1).

Optimistic Barbara felt fortunate to be employed. I was truly grateful. When my parents first tried to enter the UK job market, they were subjected to deeply offensive name-calling and even

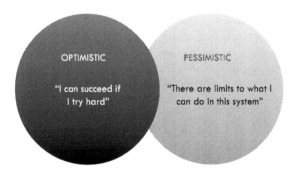

Figure 1.1 Reflections on my 1970s employment

physical violence. By the time of my supermarket chain interview, groundbreaking legislation, including the *Race Relations Acts of 1965 and 1968*, had banned discrimination in public places, ended legal discrimination in housing and made the promotion of hatred on the grounds of colour, race, ethnicity and national origins an offence. So, optimistically, there I was, a black British daughter of black immigrants able to work anywhere – except the meat counter! Would I permit a handful of ill-informed comments to get in the way of my progression in British society? No, head down, press forward, be grateful. I would work hard and succeed through my own efforts.

Pessimistic Barbara would be disappointed to discover that racism was still so embedded in British society and institutions. How sad, I would think. How sad that the organisation and structures in society and my workplace made the continuation of discrimination and preservation of white privilege inevitable. Would I always be at a disadvantage? Was this simply the way the system worked, and would I be on the wrong side of it regardless of how hard I tried?

These two perspectives resulted in an ongoing tension that has stayed with me throughout my working life. Teenage Barbara hoped that navigating the workplace was as simple as balancing sufficient capabilities and the agency to succeed. However, the reality might be that she would need to overcome systemic constraints that would obstruct her progress.

These two standpoints resonate with Cornel West's[1] "two camps" of how people interpret the reasons behind the lack of upward mobility of African Americans. One camp includes the conservative behaviourists, who focus on values and attitudes and personal agency. This camp suggests that if black people want to succeed, they only need a good work ethic, to be responsible and to try hard enough. West's other camp is composed of liberal structuralists who highlight political and economic structural constraints, discrimination in jobs and housing, poor healthcare and education. This camp typically believes that success for black people is determined by more equitable access to jobs and housing through strategies, such as targets for the number of black employees and government funding of health education and childcare programmes. West himself suggests that behaviour and structure are inseparable – the way that people act and live is shaped by the larger circumstances in which they find themselves.

Like West, I now know the reality is not individual agency or structure but far more complex and nuanced. Individual agency and broader systemic issues both have a role. What I do believe is that black people working in organisations need to develop the ability to navigate this complex reality. They must make conscious choices: Do they rail against systemic organisational issues and advocate on behalf of others, or do they keep their head down, often ignoring overt or more subtle racism, and focus on working hard believing that will ensure their personal success?

The leaders I interviewed for this book suggest that these choices were not limited to my youth. These choices are very present in the current workplace. Successful black leaders talked about the need to weigh up decisions about how to respond to perceived racial intolerance in the moment, often on a daily basis. This is an integral part of navigating race at work. An understanding of how black leaders navigate race in the moment is essential for understanding the process that black colleagues go through on a daily basis. The SCAN model describes a process used to navigate these choices.

THE SCAN: HOW BLACK PEOPLE NAVIGATE RACE IN THE MOMENT

Successful black leaders have learnt how to navigate race in the moment. This process has four stages.

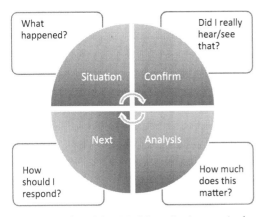

Figure 1.2 The SCAN Model: navigating race in the moment

The first stage is to observe the SITUATION. The situation might be subtle, like the look that someone gives you during a meeting or how someone interrupts or talks over you. It could be more overt, like the gorilla emoji response to your "good morning" message on MS Teams. It might be more blatant, like using the phrase "N in a woodpile." These are all recent examples from black leaders.

The next step is to CONFIRM. Did I really see or hear what I thought I did? Did they really say that? Do I want to clarify whether I did hear what I thought I heard?

The third step is ANALYSIS. "Who" did/said what matters a lot. Was it a superior, a peer, a direct report, a client? What level of importance does this person have within the organisation? What is the nature of my relationship with the individual? Is this a friend or foe? The next part of the analysis is to ascertain their intent. Did they mean it? What was the intent behind the comment? Should this person know better? Are they actually educated with regards to what they should or should not say? Has this person done/said something like this before? Is this part of a pattern? In this step many leaders also look inward: What might I have done to trigger that response in that individual in that moment?

The final step once a black leader has experienced a situation, confirmed with themselves what happened and analysed the moment, is to decide on what happens NEXT. Do you respond and call it out here and now, in the moment? Or is this something you want to pick up on later? Responses might take the form of clarification, either with the person(s) involved or witnesses to the situation, or a leader might simply ignore the situation altogether. Some leaders choose to make notes so that they can return to it later or, in the worst case, even use records to build up material that proves a pattern. The decision taken in the moment depends on a leader's energy, how they perceive a situation and, significantly, what are the consequences of their response – "what might happen if I respond to this initial trigger? What are the implications for me? How will others view me if I take action?"

Many leaders I interviewed agree that no matter what they do "next" in these situations, they can turn the events over in their minds for days, trying to make sense of what happened.

The SCAN lasts seconds. It may be partway through a meeting, in the middle of a presentation or when they are about to speak on

Zoom. Black leaders in a white workplace need to stay completely composed whilst they work through these questions, options and potential consequences.

As you might imagine, the SCAN demands a lot of mental energy. With practice, though, it becomes such a part of how black leaders function that it is an automatic response, not a conscious thought process. The SCAN – and its mental cost to black leaders – is a process we will return to in later chapters.

A GOOD TIME TO BE BLACK IN THE BRITISH WORKPLACE?

Today we see black people in all professions and at all levels. In the UK, there are black judges, black partners in law firms and consultancies, black senior police officers. Black people work in leadership positions across public and private sectors. There are black members of Parliament of all political persuasions. Organisations demonstrate their desire to be more diverse and inclusive by spending millions on equity diversity and inclusion (EDI) initiatives year in and year out. Thousands of leaders have attended bias workshops and EDI training programmes each year. More than 400 employers have ratified *The Race at Work Charter*,[2] pledging to appoint executive sponsors for race, capture ethnicity data and publicise progress, commit at board level to zero tolerance of harassment and bullying, make clear that supporting equality in the workplace is the responsibility of all leaders and managers and take action that supports ethnic minority career progression. Furthermore, white people in workplaces across the country are educating themselves on the black British experience, reading books, listening to podcasts and watching online lectures. It's a relatively good time to be black and British at work.

However.

Despite these good intentions, a mountain of evidence indicates that there is significant room for improvement. This is demonstrated in a wide range of research on the Black British workplace experience as shown in figure 1.3. According to the 2011 census,[3] black people represent 3 per cent of the UK population. In contrast, black people account for just 1 per cent of judges, senior academia, civil service and police; less than 1 per cent of journalists; and only 1.4 per cent of FTSE 100 leaders.[4]

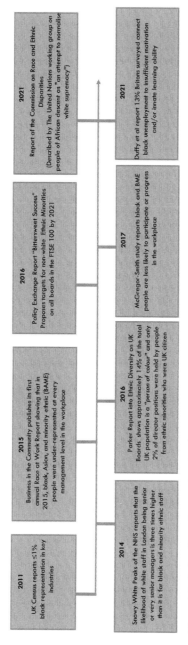

Figure 1.3 A timeline of research milestones of the black workplace experience in the UK, 2011–2021

According to Kline's[5] landmark *The Snowy White Peaks of the NHS* report on data recorded between 2008 and 2014, there was no increase in the proportion of senior and very senior managers from a black minority ethnic (BME) background in the National Health Service (NHS). In fact, the authors observed, the proportion had actually been declining since 2011. By contrast, the authors noted that the likelihood of a white person being employed as a senior or very senior manager based in London in 2014 was three times higher than for BME staff. This pattern has since been observed across parts of England.

The Snowy White Peaks of the NHS report concludes that the absence and exclusion of black managers between 2008 and 2014 appeared to be caused by discrimination in recruitment, career development and appointment processes. This was, the report suggests, despite the 2004 *Race Equality Action Plan*, a major national initiative to tackle race discrimination in the provision of health services and the employment of health service staff.

In 2015, Business in the Community published its first annual *Race at Work* report,[6] which identified that whereas one in eight of the working-age population was from a BAME background, only one in 16 were in top management positions. The report also indicated that people from a BAME background were less likely to be rated as top performers compared to their white counterparts.

The Parker Review Committee's *A Report into Ethnic Diversity on UK Boards* in 2017[7] identified that the boardrooms of Britain's leading public companies do not reflect the ethnic diversity of either the UK or the stakeholders that they represent. The committee recommended that changes are needed in the boardrooms where leadership is of utmost importance. *The Policy Exchange Report* of the same year recommended targets for non-white ethnic minorities in all FTSE 100 boards by 2021. It further proposed that FTSE 100 companies hiring for executive and non-executive board positions adopt the Rooney Rule, which requires all final interviews for top jobs to have at least one minority candidate on the list.

An extensive independent review by Baroness McGregor-Smith in 2017[8] found that not only are BME individuals in the UK less likely than white individuals to participate in the workplace, but they are also less likely to progress through it. The review identified the existence of barriers from entry right through to board level that prevent BME individuals from reaching their full potential.

A more recent study conducted in February 2021[9] (by Duffy et al., described in *The Guardian* by Robert Booth) reported that one in eight Britons (13 per cent) believe black people are more likely to be unemployed and have lower incomes because they "lack motivation or willpower." Four per cent of survey respondents believe it is because black people have "less in-born ability to learn."

Even the controversial and much disputed 2021 *Report of the Commission on Race and Ethnic Disparities*[10] stated that whilst bias, bigotry and unfairness based on race may be receding, they still have the power to deny opportunity and painfully disrupt lives. Twenty organisations and individuals who had contributed to the research withdrew their support post-publication.[11] The National Black Police Association claimed the report was a deliberate attempt at undermining lived experiences; the British Medical Association rejected the argument that structural race inequality is not a major factor that influences outcomes and life chances and the recruitment platform; Applied argued that the notion that the system was not rigged against ethnic minorities was not supported by the data. In addition, leading academics cited in the report also said that they were not properly consulted.[12]

Against this backdrop, black leaders continue to succeed.

TALKING ABOUT RACE: FILLING THE SILENCE

The start of the 2020s saw an outpouring of emotion accompanying the deaths of George Floyd and Breonna Taylor led by the Black Lives Matter movement. There is a desire to understand black people's experiences.

This desire is viewed by many black leaders with cynicism and hope in equal measure. Cynicism because we have been here before: Remember Stephen Lawrence and the MacPherson report?[13] Remember the inquiry following the 2011 Tottenham Riots?[14] The Lammy report?[15] Windrush? Numerous examples spring instantly to the minds of black people in this country. Perhaps, in this time, far away from the bottom-slapping-meat-counter days and with black lives in the news, this is the moment when white people become more aware of the lived experience of black people. Perhaps, it is not. If not, black British leaders will be left feeling even more vulnerable than before, and white leaders may feel even more vilified and thus become more defensive, doubling down on the institutions that block black professionals' progress. In the media, we will see this as a focus-pull, with reporting and entertainment backing away from systemic problems to focus instead only on the exceptional blacks and the heroic stories that demonstrate the agency and determination of black leaders. Every other black person at work will be left in the dark again.

The only way to mitigate this risk is to use the opportunity to get both black and white Brits speaking comfortably about race and racial issues.

A young black man shared an experience with me recently. To protect his career, he asked that I refer to him by a pseudonym – so, we'll call him "Kevin." Kevin is a young black British man, an Oxbridge graduate currently successfully navigating a professional services firm. The firm's black employees had set up a network for safely sharing experiences and influencing the organisation's Inclusion Agenda.

On the day in question, Kevin and a few fellow black network members were in his office, reflecting on the most recent meeting, which had been attended by a senior white partner. The conversation was in full flow and everyone was enthused and animated. Kevin's team leader – a white woman – slipped into the room, eager to hear what the fuss was about. Kevin recalled how, when she heard the senior partner had joined the meeting, the white female team leader wanted to find out more about the network and its work. She invited Kevin to present to his team at the next meeting.

"I wish I could have felt more excited," Kevin remembers. "The truth is, I was anxious. I really didn't want to speak openly about the network and the kind of discussions we had as part of it. I am the only black person in my team. They are good people, but sharing the kind of honest, frank criticisms and observations that the black network discuss in our dedicated, safe space . . . well, they aren't the topics to present when you're the only black in the team."

Despite his misgivings, Kevin pulled together a "suitably honest" presentation, focussing less on personal experience and more on statistics, particularly those relating to the firm. Also included were some of the most talked about suggestions for how the firm could be more inclusive and support the retention of black talent.

"I thought it went well," Kevin grimaces. "I'm a good presenter, and there was lots of meat to discuss. But when I finished, there was silence. Absolute, 'hear a pin drop' silence." Kevin's colleagues were terrified to speak. Terrified to offer a comment or reflection. Not even the most senior, confident team members nor the women who had spoken out on gender issues could speak. "They wouldn't even look at me. It was tense. It was silent. It was awful." Kevin remembers thanking the team before sitting down. "I still don't understand: why is it so hard for my white colleagues to fill the silence?"

If more black leaders are to enter and progress in British organisations, the silence Kevin and his white team experienced needs to be filled. Employers, leaders and managers must create environments that enable dialogue around the topic of race, where the black experience can be discussed in an empowering and restorative way for leaders, both black and white. Yes, black *and* white. It is not simple and, in truth, I sympathise with Kevin's hesitancy and the notion of not talking to white people about race. But suppose we are to build the workplace environments in which it is "okay" to talk about race? Black people have an important part to play in that process – they must, as Kevin and his network did, allow white leaders into their conversation when it matters and share our honest experiences and reflections with them. Addressing the issue of creating space to talk about being different and still ensuring there is space for all parties to be different is essential – the black experience should not be problematised and the white experience should not be vilified. "Inclusion" means an environment where "blackness"[16] and "whiteness"[17] are restorative and empowering identities.

Just as Kevin and the black network invited their white senior partner to "listen in" on their experiences, this book provides a snapshot of the everyday lives of black leaders in British workplaces. It is truth; it does not seek to judge nor avenge, only to share the black perspective on everyday occurrences.

SUCCESSFULLY NAVIGATING RACE AT WORK

The black leaders I interviewed for this book were mostly keen to reinforce the view that they do not see themselves as victims of a system. They are individuals who both consciously and unconsciously have learnt to successfully navigate race during the course of their working life. Their success can be viewed through different lenses. The behavioural lens would suggest that these black leaders have succeeded by virtue of their own agency. They have gained the appropriate qualifications, worked hard and stayed focussed. The structural lens would suggest that they have succeeded in spite of a system that is tilted against them. This structural perspective may also imply that they could have done even better had they not had to fight against an unjust system. This meant they never really achieved their full potential. It is clearly not so straightforward.

One leader interviewed for this book describes these lenses in terms of "left" and "right":

> People on the left tend to describe their success in terms of other people helping them and good fortune. Hard work as well, of course, but they largely recognise a huge amount of societal help from immediate friends and family, and the investment society makes in public services and initiatives that helped give them the framework to be successful. In contrast, people on the right tend to say they achieved their goals almost entirely through hard work, with little or no help from other people or systems.

Whatever lens or perspective a black British leader adopts, their ability to continually internally process situations and navigate race in the moment is essential to their experience of the workplace.

This chapter has explained how black people navigate race once in the workplace. Chapter 2 takes us back a stage to reveal the upbringing and educational experiences that form the black person who shows up at work.

KEY TAKEAWAYS

- Black leaders learn to navigate structural constraints and behavioural expectations in the workplace
- Black leaders continually use the SCAN process to decide how to navigate race in the moment at work
- Numerous studies have identified the challenges facing black workers and the inequitable nature of UK workplaces – yet black leaders continue to succeed, often against all the odds
- Black leaders and their white colleagues are still uncomfortable talking about race in the workplace

QUESTIONS FOR REFLECTION

- How do you see the pace of change in your organisation in relation to the inclusion of black workers?
- Do you have the vocabulary to fill the silence in conversations around race in your workplace?
- What are your reflections on black leaders' need to continually SCAN?

NOTES

1 West, C. (2001). *Race Matters*. New York: Vintage Books.
2 Business in the Community. *Race at Work Charter*. www.bitc.org.uk/post_tag/race-at-work-charter/ [Last accessed 20 July 2021].
3 2011 Census. (2017, February). *Office for National Statistics; National Records of Scotland; Northern Ireland Statistics and Research Agency (2017): 2011 Census Aggregate Data. UK Data Service*. https://www.ons.gov.uk/census/2011census.
4 Community, BiT. (2020). *Black Voices Report*. www.bitc.org.uk/report/race-at-work-black-voices-report/ [Last accessed 11 April 2021].
5 Kline, R. (2014). *The "Snowy White Peaks" of the NHS: A Survey of Discrimination in Governance and Leadership and the Potential Impact on Patient Care in London and England*. Middlesex University. www.mdx.ac.uk/__data/assets/pdf_file/0015/50190/The-snowy-white-peaks-of-the-NHS.pdf.pdf [Last accessed 13 April 2021].
6 Business in the Community. (2015). *Race at Work*. www.bitc.org.uk/report/race-at-work-2015/ [Last accessed 20 July 2021].
7 Sir Parker, J. (2017). *The Parker Review: A Report into the Ethnic Diversity of UK Boards*. London: The Parker Review Committee.
8 McGregor-Smith, R. (2017). *Race in the Workplace: The McGregor-Smith Review*. UK Government. https://assets.publishing.service.gov.uk/government/uploads/system/uploads/attachment_data/file/594336/race-in-workplace-mcgregor-smith-review.pdf [Last accessed 11 April 2021].
9 Duffey, B. et al. (2021). *Unequal Britain Attitudes to Inequalities After Covid-19*. London: The Policy Institute at Kings College; Booth, R. (2021, February 25). Job Losses in Pandemic Due to Performance Issues, Say Nearly Half of Britons. *The Guardian*. www.theguardian.com/inequality/2021/feb/25/job-losses-in-pandemic-due-to-performance-issues-say-nearly-half-of-britons [Last accessed 12 April 2021].
10 Commission on Race and Ethnic Disparities. (2021). *The Report of the Commission on Race and Ethnic Disparities*.

11 Mohdin, A. (2021). Bodies Credited in UK Race Review Distance Them-selves from Findings. *The Guardian*, April 13. www.theguardian.com/world/2021/apr/12/bodies-credited-in-uk-race-review-distance-them selves-from-findings [Last accessed 7 October 2021].

12 Mohdin, A. (2021). Experts Cited in No 10's Race Report Claim They Were not Properly Consulted. *The Guardian*, April 1. www.theguardian.com/world/2021/apr/01/experts-cited-in-no-10s-race-report-claim-they-were-not-properly-consulted [Last accessed 7 October 2021].

13 Sir Macpherson, W. (1999, >February>). *The Stephen Lawrence Inquiry Report (Command Paper)*. www.gov.uk/government/uploads/system/uploads/attachment_data/file/277111/4262.pdf [Last accessed 27 Septem-ber 2021].

14 Marcus, S., Rabbatts, H., Singh, D., & Sherlock, M. *After the Riots*. The Final Report of the Riots Communities and Victims Panel. www.salford-cvs.co.uk/sites/salfordcvs.co.uk/files/Riots-Panel-Final-Report.pdf   [Last accessed September 2021].

15 The Lammy Review: An Independent Review into the Treatment of, and Outcomes for, Black, Asian and Minority Ethnic Individuals in the Crimi-nal Justice System. (2017). www.gov.uk/government/uploads/system/uploads/attachment_data/file/643001/lammy-review-final-report.pdf.

16 Boakye, J. (2019, April 13). Smooth, Angry, Cool, Powerful: How We Talk About Blackness. *The Guardian*. www.theguardian.com/books/2019/apr/13/smooth-angry-cool-powerful-how-we-talk-about-blackness   [Last accessed 13 April 2021].

17 Frankenberg, R. (1993). *White Women Race Matters*. Minneapolis: Univer-sity of Minnesota Press.

REFERENCES AND ADDITIONAL READING

2011 Census. (2017, February). *Office for National Statistics; National Records of Scotland; Northern Ireland Statistics and Research Agency (2017): 2011 Census Aggregate Data. UK Data Service*. https://www.ons.gov.uk/census/2011cen-sus.

Andrews, K. (2018). *Back to Black: Retelling Black Radicalism for the 21st Century*. London: Zed Books Ltd.

Bell, D. (2018). *Faces at the Bottom of the Well: The Permanence of Racism*. Paris: Hachette.

Bhopal, K. (2018). *White Privilege: The Myth of a Post-Racial Society*. Bristol: Policy Press.

Boakye, J. (2019). *Black, Listed: Black British Culture Explored*. Paris: Hachette.

Boakye, J. (2019, April 13). Smooth, Angry, Cool, Powerful: How We Talk about Blackness. *The Guardian*. www.theguardian.com/books/2019/apr/13/

smooth-angry-cool-powerful-how-we-talk-about-blackness [Last accessed 13 April 2021].

Booth, R. (2021, February 25). Job Losses in Pandemic Due to Performance Issues, Say Nearly Half of Britons. *The Guardian*. www.theguardian.com/inequality/2021/feb/25/job-losses-in-pandemic-due-to-performance-issues-say-nearly-half-of-britons [Last accessed 12 April 2021].

Business in the Community. (2015). *Race at Work*. www.bitc.org.uk/report/race-at-work-2015/ [Last accessed 20 July 2021].

Business in the Community. *Race at Work Charter*. www.bitc.org.uk/post_tag/race-at-work-charter/ [Last accessed 20 July 2021].

Commission on Race and Ethnic Disparities. (2021). *The Report of the Commission on Race and Ethnic Disparities*.

Community, BiT. (2020). *Black Voices Report*. www.bitc.org.uk/report/race-at-work-black-voices-report/ [Last accessed 11 April 2021].

Duffey, B. et al. (2021). *Unequal Britain Attitudes to Inequalities After Covid-19*. London: The Policy Institute at Kings College.

Fekete, L. (2018). Lammy Review: Without Racial Justice, can there be Trust? *Race & Class* 59(3), 75–79. https://doi.org/10.1177/0306396817742074.

Frankenberg, R. (1993). *White Women Race Matters*. Minneapolis: University of Minnesota Press.

Gilroy, P. (1993). *The Black Atlantic: Modernity and Double Consciousness*. London, New York: Verso.

Kline, R. (2014). *The "Snowy White Peaks" of the NHS: A Survey of Discrimination in Governance and Leadership and the Potential Impact on Patient Care in London and England*. Middlesex University. www.mdx.ac.uk/__data/assets/pdf_file/0015/50190/The-snowy-white-peaks-of-the-NHS.pdf.pdf [Last accessed 13 April 2021].

Marcus, S., Rabbatts, H., Singh, D., & Sherlock, M. *After the Riots*. The Final Report of the Riots Communities and Victims Panel. www.salfordcvs.co.uk/sites/salfordcvs.co.uk/files/Riots-Panel-Final-Report.pdf [Last accessed September 2021].

McGregor-Smith, R. (2017). *Race in the Workplace: The McGregor-Smith Review*. UK Government. https://assets.publishing.service.gov.uk/government/uploads/system/uploads/attachment_data/file/594336/race-in-workplace-mcgregor-smith-review.pdf [Last accessed 11 April 2021].

Mohdin, A. (2021, April 13). Bodies Credited in UK Race Review Distance Themselves from Findings. *The Guardian*. www.theguardian.com/world/2021/apr/12/bodies-credited-in-uk-race-review-distance-themselves-from-findings [Last accessed 7 October 2021].

Mohdin, A. (2021, April 1). Experts Cited in No 10's Race Report Claim they were not Properly Consulted. *The Guardian*. www.theguardian.com/world/2021/apr/01/experts-cited-in-no-10s-race-report-claim-they-were-not-properly-consulted [Last accessed 7 October 2021].

Sir Macpherson, W. (1999, February). *The Stephen Lawrence Inquiry Report (Command Paper)*. www.gov.uk/government/uploads/system/uploads/attachment_data/file/277111/4262.pdf [Last accessed 27 September 2021].

Sir Parker, J. (2017). *The Parker Review: A Report into the Ethnic Diversity of UK Boards*. London: The Parker Review Committee.

The Lammy Review: An Independent Review into the Treatment of, and Outcomes for, Black, Asian and Minority Ethnic Individuals in the Criminal Justice System. (2017). www.gov.uk/government/uploads/system/uploads/attachment_data/file/643001/lammy-review-final-report.pdf.

West, C. (1991). The New Cultural Politics of Difference. In R. Ferguson et al. (Eds.), *Out There: Marginalization and Contemporary Cultures* (p. 17). Cambridge, Massachusetts: MIT Press.

West, C. (2001). *Race Matters*. New York: Vintage Books.

2

"GIRLS LIKE YOU . . ."

This chapter

- *explores the childhood experiences that impact how black leaders show up in the workplace,*
- *proposes six circumstantial influences that contribute to how black children develop into leaders,*
- *describes four categories by which to understand black leaders' educational experiences and early life and*
- *identifies how different factors act as headwinds or tailwinds in black leaders' education.*

Equally, the perceptions held by the teachers about the ability of black students played out in the way that they interacted with me, and conflicted very much with the things that I was encouraged to feel, to think, to believe in my home.

Grace Ononiwu, CBE, Senior Director,
Crown Prosecution Service

Yes, I was aware when I started out, and I'm still aware that social capital is a very real thing, and the absence of it means that you have to work a bit harder and you've got to build it up. That takes effort as well.

Jonathan Akwue, President and Global
Media Lead, Publicis Groupe

My father was a university professor; my mom was a chief pharmacist of a hospital, worked at the time in Manchester. From a

DOI: 10.4324/9781003200482-5

home perspective, I was raised by two strong black professionals who believed in their work and had a work ethic. I always had that, "Yes, you can aspire; you can do what you want to do." I think that's important there.

Paul Aliu, Head of Global Governance,
Chief Medical Office, Novartis

I was 12 and my brother was 11. . . . There was a lady, a white lady, coming towards us with a pushchair and a toddler walking next to her. We then moved to walk in single file so that we wouldn't interrupt her flow. Her toddler must've just brushed their arm against my side. She punched me in the face and used a whole lot of racist language that I won't repeat, about why we shouldn't be anywhere near her child. . . . I thought, "I'm not going to let those incidents stop me from being what I want to be."

Patricia Miller, OBE, Chief Executive,
Dorset County Hospital Foundation Trust

How do certain black children become black leaders? Why might the backgrounds and interests of black leaders be different from those of their white counterparts? This is because black British leaders do not arrive at organisations as blank canvasses. They have been conditioned by an educational system and shaped by the expectations of their families and communities. The interviews with black leaders conducted for this book revealed that the way in which a leader experienced six factors whilst growing up influenced how they showed up and their ability to be successful in a predominately white workplace. These six factors are shown in Figure 2.1.

Teacher expectations
Home life
Resilience
Identity
Versatility
Economic, social and cultural capital

Figure 2.1 THRIVE

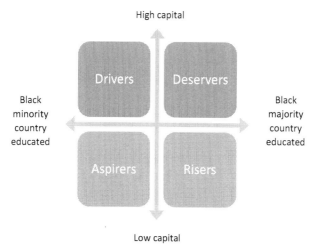

Figure 2.2 The DARD model: A framing of black British leaders

Before we examine each of the THRIVE factors in more detail, we must also consider how they are experienced by the black British leader.

The nature of the influence of THRIVE on each leader depends on two further factors: where they were educated (whether in a black majority country, in Africa, for example, or black minority country such as the UK) and the degree of their economic social and cultural capital. Four types of black leaders emerged: Drivers, Aspirers, Risers and Deservers (DARD; see Figure 2.2).

As the DARD model is based solely on research conducted for this book – there will be black leaders who do not "fit" into these boxes. Broadly speaking, however, they can be categorised as one of the four types:

- Drivers are middle-class black Britons typically of African descent. They are often second or third-generation professionals. Their parents knew how to engage with and leverage the educational system to their benefit.
- Aspirers are mainly of Caribbean descent. They typically attended state schools and were born to working-class parents

who had confidence in the educational system. Their parents were often frustrated by the leader's inability to thrive within the British educational system.

- The only Riser in this study attended a government school in their home country before winning a competitive scholarship to study in the UK. Like the Deservers (next), they possess a positive sense of self.

- Deservers are typically of African descent. When they entered the workplace, many had the same confidence and sense of entitlement as their middle-class white counterparts. They were educated privately or within government schools in their home countries.

Each type of leader experiences THRIVE factors differently; in some cases, a factor acted against them, as a **headwind**, or propelled them forwards, as a **tailwind**. Understanding the interplay of THRIVE factors and DARD in terms of headwinds and tailwinds provides deeper insight into why black leaders show up as they do in the workplace and why some find it easier than others to become leaders.

TEACHER EXPECTATIONS: A HEADWIND FOR ASPIRERS AND DRIVERS

Teacher expectations worked against the Aspirers and Drivers who were educated in the UK. Many of their school day anecdotes resonated with my own experience: Towards the end of my penultimate year of secondary school, my classmate Tracy (not her real name) told me that she had been advised by the head of German, Mrs H, to apply to the University of Oxford. Mrs H had assured Tracy she would provide her with all the necessary support.

Now, I loved German! I had just spent a month with my penfriend in Herborn, and my German had improved phenomenally. Was my German good enough for me to apply to Oxford too? I had very little understanding of exactly what "going to Oxford" meant, but if it was good enough for star pupil Tracy, Oxford sounded like a great place for me too.

So, I summoned up the confidence to find Mrs H.

Mrs H was a very unpredictable character, and there was an equal chance that she would be sympathetic and supportive or irritated and angry, so I was nervous. I remember how loud my steps seemed on the wooden floor. As I walked, I began to question whether I had any right to ask about Oxford. As I got nearer, I felt a combination of excitement and trepidation. What if Mrs H said I could apply? What if I got in? Spotting her smiling in the distance, I realised that today, I would be talking to the warm, caring Mrs H. As I approached, I noticed a touch of anxiety slip into her smile. I told her what I had heard from Tracy and asked if I could apply. My question took her by surprise.

In hindsight, Mrs H meant well. She remarked that my German was not as accurate as Tracy's, so I would need to work very hard. I animatedly promised to practice, day and night!

"To be quite honest with you, Barbara," Mrs H hesitated, ". . . girls like you . . . don't go to Oxford." It felt like a slap in the face. I think I may have taken a step back with the force of being put back in my place. I felt crushed. I did not reply; I acquiesced and walked away. I did not possess the confidence or the knowledge to respond to her comment. I knew precisely what she meant by "girls like me" – black girls from working-class backgrounds. Later, I wondered how Mrs H might have responded had I been Julie, the pearlescent girl with long brown hair who kept horses. Julie's sister had studied at Oxford – so clearly, girls like Julie go there!

I struggled to regain my confidence. I was angry for a long time. So much so that I started asking myself what the point was in focussing so heavily on my schoolwork. I was cross because I knew that the world was not a fair place, and Mrs H had given me an unkind reminder of this unfairness. I am not sure when I stopped being so angry, but by the time exams loomed ahead, I realised that if I did not get my head down and do some serious work, I would not be going to any decent university.

Perhaps 17-year-old Barbara wasn't Oxford material. But the experience of being a black Aspirer with her confidence damaged by an insensitive teacher is not unique to me. I may even have got off lightly. In his 2021 documentary *Subnormal: A British Scandal*[1] about black Caribbean children in the British educational system, Steve McQueen highlights how many of them were unnecessarily sent to educationally subnormal schools. This happened on account of a system underpinned by eugenics: the belief that white children were more intelligent than black children. Though the consequences may be different today, a black student perception problem continues.

UK research by Millard et al.[2] shows that teacher biases against black Caribbean boys affect teacher assessment outcomes and disciplinary measures such as school exclusions. US research by Gershenson et al.[3] indicates that black teachers' expectations for black students are as much as 30 to 40 per cent higher than those of non-black teachers. The effects of this are more significant for black male students than for black female students. In the UK, research by Vincent et al.[4] suggests that black middle-class students attain fewer GCSE qualifications during compulsory schooling in the UK than their white middle-class counterparts. A 2016 study from the Universities and Colleges Admissions Service[5] suggests there is no systemic bias against ethnic minorities in higher education admissions. However, as Gary Loke[6] from the Equality Challenge Unit highlighted later that year, that there remained a considerable gap between the proportions of white British students awarded a 2:1[7] or higher upon graduation compared to British students from minority ethnic backgrounds – so it would appear that a systemic bias continues to operate.

Within the school system, black Caribbean boys are nearly four times more likely to receive a permanent school exclusion than the school population as a whole.[8] Black children are also twice as likely to be identified with special educational needs.[9] These statistics bring me back to the issue of the impact of both individual agency and structural issues discussed in Chapter 1. To what extent is the performance of black students connected to a lack of individual agency? To what extent is there something systemic within the educational system that accounts for these differences?

My experience of being underestimated is still being played out in schools today. One of the most disappointing examples I have heard came in 2018 from a 16-year-old black girl at my daughter's school. Despite being a well-behaved student, with a string of A★ grades at GCSE level, her chemistry teacher scoffed and laughed at her desire to become a doctor: "What, you, medicine?" This comment was more subtle than Mrs H's, but the meaning was the same.

Another student told me, "I don't experience racism at school, except for the fact that the teachers always underestimate me." This is the crux of the issue: Black children can become conditioned by teacher underestimation. As in the case of this 16-year-old, with positive parental support, many children can rise above teacher expectations. For others, low expectations can lead to a loss of confidence and act as a real limitation.

Fortunately, for those who became leaders in organisations, low teacher expectations did not represent a straitjacket. They had learnt that low expectations are could either be ignored or serve as a challenge to be overcome. My own experience taught me resilience, and when I graduated and went to work, I was ready to ignore or exceed the expectations of those around me. I was, however, also tired – tired of low expectations and being told what I could not do.

Teacher expectations were a strong theme in the interviews. Whilst most recollections reflected my own, some leaders also acknowledged the teachers who did see and encourage the talent in young black students. In their fortunate cases, teacher expectations served as a tailwind to their success. Additionally, the younger black professionals we will meet in Chapter 10 referred often to positive teacher support. Notably, teacher expectations were discussed far more often by senior Aspirers and Drivers than by all other leaders.

HOME LIFE: A TAILWIND FOR ALL

Tailwinds in the system offer Aspirers and Drivers some support to counterbalance the headwinds caused by the school system and society. For example, my parents expected me to achieve. They set an extremely high value to education and encouraged and affirmed academic success in the ways that they knew best.

"Yuh haf fe study yuh book" was the constant refrain. I distinctly remember being five years old, in primary school, when children were still awarded a class position based on their performance on the end-of-year tests. In my first year, I ranked second best! My teacher told me that this was a considerable achievement, and I ran home to tell my parents. But to them, it was not a cause for celebration. Second place is good, but why had I not achieved first place? The disappointment was palpable. It was even more marked when I earned "only" fifth place the following year. Their response was discouraging for my six-year-old self, but it was a clear lesson on what mattered in life. Receiving a school report throughout my school life was always accompanied by trepidation. You went to school to *be* the best, not to *do* your best.

As with many of the leaders I spoke with, my parents often reminded me that they had come to this country to make a life for themselves and their children. The only way to achieve that was through education. To this end, they were always concerned about the "company you keep." We were coached not to allow any of our well-meaning but unambitious white friends to hold us back. These white people could get on very well by being second best. There would always be jobs and opportunities for average white children. Average was not an option for us. My parents had a certain Jamaican tough love, always-stick-never-carrot way of encouraging us to learn. Like many of the leaders I spoke to, I leaned into these parental expectations.

Amongst the leaders interviewed, high parental expectations were drivers for success for leaders across all four groups. For example, Paul Aliu, a successful pharmaceutical professional and Driver, shared how his professional African and Caribbean parents expected nothing less than excellence. Whilst it is still very much a tailwind for other types of leaders, Aspirers of Caribbean origin felt its effects far less than Paul – high expectations around educational attainment were often less pronounced where a leader's parents were not professionals.

A second element of home life is parents' engagement with the educational system. Parental engagement took many forms. Although lacking any social capital, my parents were engaged with the British education system to the extent that they understood it. I passed the 11-plus, the grammar school entry exam, which creamed off the top 10 per cent of children, without receiving any specific preparation – if there was any preparation to be done, my parents were not aware of it. I arrived at school and took the test.

We moved to a new house in Coventry the summer before I was due to start secondary school, only to find that there was no space for me in the local grammar school. My father was not going to accept this – he "did not come to this country to have his children offered a second-class education." My father visited the City

Council offices daily, demanding to meet with the person in charge of school place allocation. He even rejected an offer of a place for me at an outstanding comprehensive school outside our home catchment area, instead insisting on telephoning the Council's offices until they eventually agreed to transfer my grammar school place to Coventry.

Parental engagement is one of the critical elements in the success of children in school. In the case of black parents, this involvement may require confidence in challenging teachers and taking up any issues within the school hierarchy. This can be particularly important where issues of race or stereotyping need to be addressed.

One particular parents' evening is indelibly etched in my mind. Up to that point, my Year 3 daughter had had a relatively uneventful journey at her predominantly white village school. On the parent's evening in question, I met one of her teachers who was new to the school. The teacher had never met me before and did not know my family. There was an air of condescension in her voice throughout the exchange, which I ignored. My daughter's schoolwork was excellent, yes. And, yes, she has friends and plays well with them. So it's as if from nowhere, then, that I hear her say, "You do know that your daughter is a very aggressive little girl."

I felt my body heating up. It was one of those moments when I was grateful that I could not be seen to blush! I SCANned. I put on the face of the intellectual, curious black mother. Any sign of anger would play into her stereotype.

"How does that manifest itself?" I tried to clarify. The teacher struggled to respond, unable to recollect any specific instances. How could she make such a sweeping statement without particular examples? I did not tell my daughter about what her teacher had said.

I called the headmistress the following morning. I told her I was shocked at the language being used to describe my daughter, and I was unclear why her "aggression" had not been brought to my notice before. Why was I not informed? Could we have worked on this together? The headmistress said immediately, there is no evidence of any aggression from your daughter, ever. She went on to express her disappointment that a staff member would use such a word to describe a child. She would speak to the teacher and ask her to provide a full explanation and apologise. We received an apology the same day.

I watched that teacher very carefully. I listened to what my daughter said about her. I hope that I was able to protect her from a negative school experience.

A 2012 study by Gillborn[10] and colleagues of the Educational Strategies of Black Middle Classes identified that black parents were concerned and actively involved in education, supporting their children through the educational system by initiating meetings with teachers and establishing a dialogue of equals. The study also identified that the black middle class recognise the dangers of more subtle and coded forms of racism within the British school system. They experience and are aware of teacher expectations and the teachers' tendency to stereotype black children. Unlike many of their white middle-class friends, the black middle class do not assume an entitlement to a good education.

RESILIENCE: AN IMPORTANT TAILWIND FOR ASPIRERS

Many of the leaders interviewed made reference to an inner drive and determination to succeed that they had experienced before entering the workplace. David Lammy, a member of Parliament (MP), for example, spoke about his inquisitiveness and determination as a young boy.

As an MP, David is passionate about representing and supporting his community. In our conversation, I experienced David as vibrant, driven, sensitive and full of humility and gratitude for how his life had evolved. David grew up in Tottenham but left London when he was awarded a choral scholarship at the Kings School in Peterborough. In our conversation, he described how, from a young age, he was an ambitious kind of chap, very precocious, someone who worked hard and wanted to succeed. David always had a strong work ethic, and he found that there were always people who would help him. He also had a nearly insatiable thirst for knowledge.

In many ways, David's experience was similar to my own; I grew up in a home where, for many years, the only book I saw in the house was the King James Version of the Bible. We simply did not have any other books at home. My insatiable desire for information can be traced back to three sources. First, my father, illiterate on account of a childhood accident, always asked me to read the newspaper to him. From this, I developed a genuine interest in current affairs and possessed an in-depth understanding of the world according to the *Daily Mirror*. Second, when I was about ten years old, my mother bought a set of US encyclopaedias called *Childcraft*. There were 15 volumes, and I set about being conversant with the content of all of them. Finally, there was Sunday school, where we were encouraged to learn and recite verses and even whole chapters from the Bible. As a family, we went to church three times on a Sunday, with prayer meeting on Tuesday, Bible study on Thursday and youth meeting on Saturday. Although a lapsed churchgoer, I recognise now how the church helped train my mind and provided me with education, discipline and resilience.

Again, this experience is not unique to me – the black church played a vital role in the upbringing of many of the leaders I interviewed. This association between the black church and educational aspirations and achievements has been demonstrated in recent research.[11]

Another aspect of resilience was the black leader's ability to ignore everyday racism. For Derek Bruce, a senior HR leader, one particular memory stands out: Members of the local police force visited Derek's class to discuss fighting crime and becoming a policeman. The police officers invited the children to join in in acting out a crime scenario. First, they needed "policemen." Derek's hand shot up. The policeman chose two white kids.

"Then," Derek recalls, "They needed somebody to volunteer to be a 'criminal.'" Derek did not raise his hand. Without missing a beat, the policeman pointed straight at Derek. Years later, he is incredulous. "There's a class of thirty kids, one of whom is black, and he just happened to pick that black kid to be the baddie?!" Interestingly, Derek thought very little of it at the time. Racism had become subtle and normalised in the school to the extent that Derek did not even notice it.

As a young schoolboy, Derek was a victim of stereotypes of black children in society more generally. Black boys, in particular, are associated with a stereotype that is violent, disrespectful, hypersexual unintelligent[12] and, as Derek learnt, criminal.[13] These stereotypes naturally transfer into the school environment and are subtly reinforced by incidents like this one. Derek navigated the incident by choosing to stay resilient and ignore it.

IDENTITY: A TAILWIND FOR DESERVERS AND RISERS

The black leaders who had been educated in a black majority country had a strong and positive sense of their identity and history (in contrast to many of the black leaders educated in the UK). These Deservers had no experience of an educational system in which they had to deal with negative stereotypes, low expectations and everyday racism. The Deserver leaders interviewed for this book had refreshingly ordinary stories of their schooling – no tales of racism or trauma, of navigating a hostile environment as an outsider. To them, skin colour did not play any role in their educational prospects, and thus, as children, they grew up confident in their skin colour and cultural heritage. Consequently, they entered the workplace possessing a positive sense of self and often unbridled confidence. These leaders believed that they could make it, regardless of where in the world they were.

However, Deservers are not immune to social hierarchies. Research for this book revealed that these hierarchies may not be based on skin colour but are often related to money and connections.

A recent Oxbridge graduate, a Driver, told me of his experience of this. In his first term at university, he attended an event at the college's African Caribbean society. The event was dominated by Deservers. The Driver made it two feet through the door before one of the black Deserver students asked, "Who is your father?"

Puzzled, he replied with his father's name.

"No, WHO is your father? What does he do?"

The Deserver was trying to identify his father's position in the hierarchy of the African country he came from. "Is he a governor? Does he own a business? A law firm?"

Just like the Deserver profile discussed earlier in this chapter, many of these black Oxbridge students were educated primarily in an African country or at an expensive private school outside their native country. These student Deservers had arrived at university with pride, confidence and the same high expectations as their white counterparts. They had been brought up with a positive self-image and a strong sense of identity. They were proud of the history and culture of their home countries. They "knew" intrinsically that they deserved an Oxbridge education. These Deserver students at the

African Caribbean event had the same confidence that I sensed from leaders who had no experience of the UK's educational system.

This sense of confidence was also evident in the case of the one Riser interviewed for this book.

VERSATILITY: A TAILWIND FOR ASPIRERS, DRIVERS

"Versatility" in this context describes the ability to get along with and connect with people who are different to yourself – often white people. Many of the successful leaders educated in Britain attended predominantly white schools. As a result, they understood how to navigate school life as a visibly different outsider. The experience also provided them with an early grasp of the subtleties of navigating in a primarily white, often middle-class setting.

The Aspirers and Drivers interviewed for this book demonstrate a particular affinity for versatility, and specifically, knowing how to get along with white colleagues.

Paul Cleal, OBE, a former partner of PricewaterhouseCoopers (PwC), believes that the strategy he developed in school also prepared him for working alongside white people once he entered the workplace. Paul is a mixed-race man of Cameroonian and English parentage. Speaking over Zoom, Paul struck me as a calm, reflective leader. He was very aware that his success was due both to his hard work and the help he had received from other people. Reflecting on his move from a mixed primary school to an all-white secondary school, Paul recognises that he had to find a way of navigating his colour without entirely giving up his authenticity.

"One of my big moments in my life was when I got a scholarship to a good school," he recalls. "The move took me away from the social group of people that I'd grown up with in primary school and who lived in my street in Croydon, and sort of transplanted me into a different society.

"I found it incredibly difficult for a couple of years. At the age of 11, I get to this middle-class school, almost entirely white people. I was certainly the only black person in the school. I remember this guy came up on the first day and touched my face to see if the colour came off!"

Paul struggled to settle in – until a pivotal moment when he decided that if his school could not accept him for who he was, he would need to be brave enough to leave. Actively being authentic meant that Paul chose to stay at the school on his terms. He ultimately thrived in that environment. Paul learnt that as a mixed-race boy, he could find a way to fit in. It would take time, and he would want to fit in on his terms, but slowly he could find his place.

"What you learn in terms of sociability and how you fit into society. How you make yourself relevant and important to other people, liked, all those things, I think I learned a lot about that quite early on in my life, and I learnt a lot of that because of my colour."

This versatility to fit in proved important in his career. Like many of the successful black leaders, Paul was able to do this without the cost of giving away his own authenticity.

Many of the black leaders used this versatility to help them progress through school. One such example came from a senior executive at a global finance company. Of Jamaican parentage, he grew up in a majority-white area in Hertfordshire. His ability to make people feel at ease was an essential tool in his personal mission to show white people that black boys were "not all the same."

"In school, I dated white English girls, and if they had racist fathers, I'd be trying to show the father actually, you know what, I'm a really good guy." He was always on his best behaviour, and this could be tiring. He also told a lot of jokes and so was regarded as affable and funny.

Reflecting on their experiences of secondary school, many of the leaders interviewed chose simply "not to get involved" in conversations where issues of race were discussed.

"There was no one to back me up," one leader shared. "It was much easier to act like you were not different at all."

None of the strategies discussed were overtly suggested by parents or peers – these were ways in which the leaders were conditioned to navigate their time at school successfully. We will examine how some of these behaviours developed and played out in the workplace in Section 2 of this book.

ECONOMIC, SOCIAL AND CULTURAL CAPITAL: ASPIRERS NAVIGATING THE HEADWIND OF BEING BOTH BLACK AND WORKING CLASS

I had never seen myself as poor or underprivileged until I moved to my all-white, middle-class, all-girls grammar school. I recall a massive disagreement with one of my new white friends, who insisted that she had a bath every evening. This was impossible, I argued. In our house, the immersion heater was put on to heat the water *only* on Fridays. As far as I knew, no one could afford to bathe every day! I soon understood that I was one of the most impoverished children in the class, lacking both money and – as I see now, in hindsight – some of the fundamental social understanding needed to succeed in that kind of middle-class environment. I recall the shame of being the only person in our year to receive free school meals. My friends went to theatres and museums. Some even went on foreign holidays. Their parents had good jobs that provided them with connections that could help them to succeed in life. I realised that there was a whole other way of life of which I had no understanding or access. I lacked what sociologist Pierre Bourdieu[14] calls "economic, social and cultural capital."

Bourdieu was interested in how power dynamics play out in society. He proposed that individuals from different social groups were different from each other in relation to three forms of capital: social, cultural and economic. Economic capital was about the possession of money and finances, social capital was about relationships and connections and cultural capital was about knowledge skills and education.

My parents could have done things differently if they knew what was available and if they knew that, in many cases, they cost very little. Some parents knew that gaining cultural capital does not have to be totally dependent on economic capital. Paul Cleal, OBE, told me how his white mother was good at encouraging curiosity. "I got taken to every bloody museum in London from age five onwards. The school I went to might have been no good at all, but she made up for it by educating me at home and taking me to the Science Museum, Tower of London, you name it. All free, of course, anyone could have done it."

Few of the leaders interviewed for this book left school possessing the social capital required to succeed in British corporate life. Even the Deservers lacked contacts within UK companies. Levels of cultural capital depended on the type of school attended. The three privately educated leaders possessed the most cultural capital.

There is no single black British leader with educational and family experience. Consequently, black leaders enter the workplace having had a range of different influences. However, there are factors that they have in common. The UK-educated black leaders interviewed for this book were able to successfully navigate the educational system despite the many obstacles they encountered. This was due to high family expectations, an inner drive to succeed and their ability to understand how to function in a primarily white environment. They were able to make it despite being educated within a system in which their identity was often not affirmed. Those educated in a majority-black country possessed an assuredness and confidence that came from being educated in a system where skin colour was not an issue. Whilst some groups possessed economic and cultural capital, most types lacked the social capital that many of their white counterparts possessed.

Building on the understanding of how leaders navigate race in the moment (Chapter 1) and how they learn to navigate race as they grow up, Chapter 3 will peel away a further layer to reveal how black leaders navigate everyday racism.

KEY TAKEAWAYS

- Drivers, Deservers, Aspirers and Risers are helpful ways of loosely categorising black leaders
- Leaders' experiences of THRIVE factors – Teacher expectations, Home life, Resilience, Identity, Versatility and Economic circumstances – influence how they show up at work
- Leaders educated in majority-black countries possessed greater confidence in their identities and their ability to succeed than those educated in the UK

QUESTIONS FOR REFLECTION

- How would you describe your experience of school?
- What do you assume about your colleagues' experiences of growing up?
- How did your family life contribute to your success in later life?
- What were the headwinds and tailwinds that you experienced when growing up?
- What elements of social, economic or cultural capital were you exposed to as a child?

NOTES

1 Shannon, L. (2021). *Subnormal: A British Scandal* [Film]. Turbine Studios. https://letterboxd.com/film/subnormal-a-british-scandal/.

2 Millard, W., Bowen-Viner, K., Baars, S., Trethewey, A., & Menzies, L. (2018). *Boys on Track: Improving Support for Black Caribbean and Free School Meal-Eligible White Boys in London*. LKM Co. https://cfey.org/wp-content/uploads/2018/12/LKMco-and-GLA-Boys-on-Track-FINAL-version-for-web.pdf.

3 Gershenson, S., Holt, S. B., & Papageorge, N. W. (2016, June). Who Believes in Me? The Effect of Student – Teacher Demographic Match on Teacher Expectations. *Economics of Education Review* 52, 209–224. www.sciencedirect.com/science/article/abs/pii/S0272775715300959 [Last accessed 14 April 2021].

4 Vincent, C., Rollock, N., Ball, S., & Gillborn, D. (2012). Being Strategic, Being Watchful, Being Determined: Black Middle-Class Parents and Schooling. *British Journal of Sociology of Education* 33(3), 337–354.

5 UCAS. (2016). *Unconscious Bias Report*. www.ucas.com/file/74801/download?token=M80wi05k.

6 Loke, G. (2015). Does Ethnicity Influence Likelihood of Admission to University? *Times Higher Education*. www.timeshighereducation.com/blog/does-ethnicity-influence-likelihood-admission-university#survey-answer.

7 UK universities award degrees at 4 grades. First Class, Upper Second Class (2:1), Lower second class (2:2) and Third Class.

8 Demie, F., & McLean, C. (2007). Raising the Achievement of African Heritage Pupils: A Case Study of Good Practice in British Schools. *Educational Studies* 33(4), 415–434.

9 Strand, S., & Lindorff, A. (2018). *Ethnic Disproportionality in the Identification of Special Educational Needs (SEN) in England: Extent, Causes and Consequences*. The University of Oxford. www.education.ox.ac.uk/wp-content/uploads/2018/08/Executive-Summary_2018-12-20.pdf [Last accessed 14 April 2021].

10 Gillborn, D., Rollock, N., Vincent, C., & Ball, S. J. (2012). 'You Got a Pass, So What More Do You Want?': Race, Class and Gender Intersections in the Educational Experiences of the Black Middle Class. *Race Ethnicity and Education* 15(1), 121–139.

11 Dumangane, C. Jr. (2017). The Significance of Faith for Black Men's Educational Aspirations. *British Educational Research Journal* 43(5), 875–903.

12 Martino, W., & Mayenn, B. (2001). *What About the Boys?: Issues of Masculinity in Schools*. Buckingham: Open University Press.

13 Tomlinson, S. (2005). *Education in a Post-Welfare Society*. Second Edition. Maidenhead: Open University Press.

14 Bourdieu, P. (1984). *Distinction: A Social Critique of the Judgement of Taste*. London: Routledge.

REFERENCES AND ADDITIONAL READING

Bourdieu, P. (1984). *Distinction: A Social Critique of the Judgement of Taste*. London: Routledge.

Byfield, C. (2008). The Impact of Religion on the Educational Achievement of Black Boys: A UK and USA Study. *British Journal of Sociology of Education* 29(2), 189–199.

Demi, F. (2021). The Experience of Black Caribbean Pupils in School Exclusion in England. *Educational Review* 73(1), 55–70.

Demie, F. (2019). Raising Achievement of Black Caribbean Pupils: Good Practice for Developing Leadership Capacity and Workforce Diversity in Schools. *School Leadership & Management* 39(1), 5–25.

Demie, F., & McLean, C. (2007). Raising the Achievement of African Heritage Pupils: A Case Study of Good Practice in British Schools. *Educational Studies* 33(4), 415–434.

Dumangane, Jr. C. (2017). The Significance of Faith for Black Men's Educational Aspirations. *British Educational Research Journal* 43(5), 875–903.

Gershenson, S., Holt, S. B., & Papageorge, N. W. (2016, June). Who Believes in Me? The Effect of Student – Teacher Demographic Match on Teacher Expectations. *Economics of Education Review* 52, 209–224. www.sciencedirect.com/science/article/abs/pii/S0272775715300959 [Last accessed 14 April 2021].

Gillborn, D. (2008). *Racism and Education: Coincidence or Conspiracy?* London: Routledge.

Gillborn, D., Rollock, N., Vincent, C., & Ball, S. J. (2012). 'You Got a Pass, So What More Do You Want?': Race, Class and Gender Intersections in the Educational Experiences of the Black Middle Class. *Race Ethnicity and Education* 15(1), 121–139.

Loke, G. (2015). Does Ethnicity Influence Likelihood of Admission to University? *Times Higher Education*. www.timeshighereducation.com/blog/does-ethnicity-influence-likelihood-admission-university#survey-answer [Last accessed 14 April 2021].

Martino, W., & Mayenn, B. (2001). *What About the Boys?: Issues of Masculinity in Schools*. Buckingham: Open University Press.

Millard, W., Bowen-Viner, K., Baars, S., Trethewey, A., & Menzies, L. (2018). *Boys on Track: Improving Support for Black Caribbean and Free School Meal-Eligible White Boys in London*. LKM Co. https://cfey.org/wp-content/uploads/2018/12/LKMco-and-GLA-Boys-on-Track-FINAL-version-for-web.pdf [Last accessed 14 April 2021].

Rollock, N., Gillborn, D., Vincent, C., & Ball, S. J. (2014). *The Colour of Class: The Educational Strategies of the Black Middle Classes*. Abingdon and New York: Routledge.

Strand, S., & Lindorff, A. (2018). *Ethnic Disproportionality in the Identification of Special Educational Needs (SEN) in England: Extent, Causes and Consequences.* The University of Oxford. www.education.ox.ac.uk/wp-content/uploads/2018/08/Executive-Summary_2018-12-20.pdf [Last accessed 14 April 2021].

Tomlinson, S. (2005). *Education in a Post-Welfare Society.* Second Edition. Maidenhead: Open University Press.

UCAS. (2016). *Unconscious Bias Report.* www.ucas.com/file/74801/download?token=M80wi05k [Last accessed 20 July 2021].

Vincent, C., Rollock, N., Ball, S., & Gillborn, D. (2012). Being Strategic, Being Watchful, Being Determined: Black Middle-Class Parents and Schooling. *British Journal of Sociology of Education* 33(3), 337–354.

Youdell, D. (2003). Identity Traps or How Black [1] Students Fail: The Interactions between Biographical, Sub-Cultural, and Learner Identities. *British Journal of Sociology of Education* 24(1), 3–20.

"THIS IS THE QUEUE FOR BUSINESS CLASS"

This chapter

- *describes the "Jolts" that remind black leaders of their race at work,*
- *introduces five categories of racial experiences in the workplace and*
- *examines the impact of workplace experiences and SCANning on black leaders.*

I wonder if the person who is a non-person of colour just goes, "Oh, okay, I didn't get the job," and that's it, done, and they stop thinking about it. Whereas I know, I'd be like, "Was it this? Was it that? Was it this?"

Derek Bruce, Head of Leadership
Development, Signify

They'd gone to a Grad Prix racetrack. Part of the Away Day was that they had to remove the tires of the car very quickly like they do in racing. One of his white colleagues had said to him, "Oh, you should be good at this."

Anon, Senior Executive,
Public Relations

I honestly think for most of the straight white men that I encounter, it's [racism] not an active thing. Meaning there are a few that actively go out to do something wrong, for sure. That happens. I think most of them are just living in the world, trying to do the best they can. They've gotten these stereotypes,

DOI: 10.4324/9781003200482-6

whether they come from movies, from their parents, their communities or schools, whatever.

> Michael Sherman, Chief Strategy and
> Transformation Officer, BT

All the things which they take for granted and all the things, you know, which are simple, like you move into a new house, how are the neighbours going to react? You walk into a shop in a different area, how are the shopkeepers going to react? You check into a hotel in the middle of nowhere, are you going to get hassle? You get a brand new car which is worth £50,000, are you going to be stopped by police yet again and have to prove it's your car?

> Derek Bruce, Head of Leadership
> Development, Signify

From experience, I find people don't necessarily say they don't like you, or they're racist or whatever it is, but every so often they will say something that, I don't know, that gives an insight to a bias around your blackness.

> Lorna Matty, People Development
> Manager, Toyota

INTRODUCING THE JOLT

A plethora of challenges and realities greet people as they enter the world of professional work: They want to do well, impress those around them and be recognised for their performance. They understand that there are organisational cultures of which they need to be cognizant, and they need to be prepared to adapt to them. Most people accept that there are corporate politics to be understood and navigated.

An additional challenge exists for non-white leaders and colleagues: they must also cope with the daily pressure of their work often being subject to more scrutiny. Minorities are hypervisible. Black leaders know they have to be better to be in with a chance of being equal in these workspaces. Black leaders talk about going about their daily work, aware of all these pressures. This is something that is accepted and often not even thought about on a conscious level.

However comfortable they may become in their workplace, there are times when black people are suddenly reminded that they are different from the majority. The shock often comes at a moment when they are absorbed in performing and achieving, and they are abruptly shocked out of any perception they may have had that their colour might not be a significant issue for those around them. Such incidents were reported by many of the leaders in this study. I call this the Jolt. The Jolt is an unexpected moment when a sudden racial incident or comment shifts the unconscious sense of difference of being an outsider to the conscious.

For many, the Jolt may be a traumatic experience. They can be events that cause actual emotional injury. According to Bryant-Davis and Ocampo,[1] racist incidents perpetrated on an individual would fit the standard definition of trauma regardless of the motivation. Trauma is an experience or repeated event that completely overwhelms an individual's ability to cope.[2]

In the UK, racism has become more subtle and often covert. Bryant-Davis and Ocampo suggest that subtle racism can be especially confusing for black people because they are born into them and are not taught the tools of critical thinking needed to question or even recognise them. Being targeted by someone who you previously trusted can be particularly traumatising. This could include a boss or friend. The severity of the trauma can be increased when the incident happens in public. It is important to recognise that black people do feel this racism and are affected by it. Confusion may arise in the black leader due to their inability to name what is happening.

It was often well into our interviews that the black leaders interviewed for this book brought up such incidents. Many said that they had tried to forget about them, to disconnect from them. When they did talk about these incidents, I noticed a deep sense of hurt and even anger remained, even though years may have passed. As the impact is long-lasting, for some black people, such racist incidents are not far from their consciousness. Consequently, when an unexpected incident occurs, black people are often primed for a traumatic response.[3] This may be one of the reasons why black people are accused of oversensitivity in relation to their response to racist incidents.

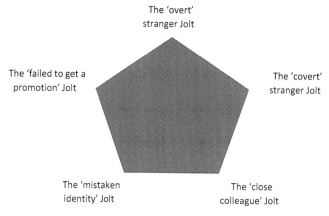

Figure 3.1 The five kinds of *Jolts*

When the Jolt happens, many leaders find they can carry out the SCAN discussed in Chapter 1. They can make a considered response. For others, the shock is such that they are frozen, unable to respond. For others, it is an incident to be repressed or forgotten as they move on with their careers. The black leaders I spoke to do not see themselves as victims of the Jolts. These are simply another set of experiences that they take in their stride on their leadership journey.

Based on the research for this book, there are five types of Jolts most black leaders experience at work (Figure 3.1).

THE "OVERT" STRANGER JOLT

Mark is a black professional who spent many years in large corporates. He now runs his own successful design company. He is experienced and confident when he pitches for work. As with all design companies, he does not always win the business. Whether he wins or loses, he typically receives feedback on the reasons for this. These responses usually seem sufficiently objective; he did not demonstrate that he fully understood the brief, they thought that other design companies had a superior visual or he was good but too expensive! Mark had not been particularly conscious of his colour in relation to his work. He just happened to be a black designer. In many ways, Mark felt he was just like many of his clients. He had a house in a prosperous suburb, enjoyed quality foreign holidays and cared deeply about his children's education.

Mark had been working on a significant pitch for a medium-sized company. He had been communicating with the managing director. The discussions were productive, and they successfully moved the project along without meeting in person. In addition to discussing the project, they built up a good rapport sharing their mutual love of cricket. Mark had the sense that he had a good chance of winning this piece of work. The day of the face-to-face pitch arrived. Mark got ready in his usual way: smart suit, no tie. He arrived at the client's office 30 minutes before his appointment. As he walked in, the receptionist looked at him with what he thought was an apologetic look. Was this really a strange look, or was he just a bit nervous? Something did not feel right, but he worked hard to set aside that feeling and sat down. He was eventually ushered into a room to meet the managing director.

The managing director walked into the office. He did not look Mark in the eye but looked past him as he said, "Yes, do you know what? I've had a change of mind. I want to give this to one of my own."

"Well, what do you mean?" Mark asked.

"Well, yes, you know, I want to do this with one of my own. I don't want to work with you." It felt like everything that happened next occurred in slow motion. Mark looked at the managing director, shocked. He wanted to respond, but a quick SCAN suggested otherwise – there was no point. The managing director owned the company, and it was his decision. He turned around and left the room. He decided that he would attempt to charge for the work he had done. There was nothing more to do. As he walked out, the receptionist said how sorry she was.

Mark did not talk to anyone about this incident. He pushed all thoughts about that day to the back of his mind. It was only in the light of the conversations around the death of George Floyd that Mark was able to share what had happened with his close family. As he spoke to them about the incident, he realised how much he had tried to suppress the memories of that experience.

These kinds of Jolts can result in a severe knock to the leader's confidence. The danger for Mark is that each time he loses a pitch, he wonders whether this might be on account of his race.

Mark has not talked about his experience with his white friends because he was deeply embarrassed and ashamed by what had happened. He wanted to forget about it and move on. Some black leaders may be prepared to talk about such Jolts, others may have experienced them as traumatic and not want to discuss them further.

THE "COVERT" STRANGER JOLT

"Are you in the right queue? They called business class." My scenario would be something like this. I've been abroad for a week working with a fabulous group of participants on a leadership programme. During that week, I was probably the only black face in the hotel and the only black face in the classroom. After the initial look of surprise when I check in at reception, the hotel staff are accommodating, especially once they realise I am one of the lead facilitators. I spend a fantastic week with the group, and I leave on Friday, exhausted but energised. I get to the airport and am suddenly reminded that I am a black lady, a second-class citizen – and could not possibly be in the correct queue! This experience only occurs when I am travelling alone.

Whenever I approached accompanied by a white man or white woman, and there is never an issue. Alongside my white colleagues, I become an honorary white and am therefore elevated to first-class status.

I thought this experience was unique to me, the five-foot-three black lady travelling alone. Then I spoke with Derek Bruce. Derek is a senior executive at an international technology company. His parents are from Barbados. He is tall and has an elegant demeanour, and strikes me as combining confidence with a positive and thoughtful manner. His career in HR has taken him from global insurance to international retail, and he is now responsible for a spin-off of a technology organisation. He spends a lot of time at airports, travelling alone and invariably travels business class. Derek told me about his experience when travelling alone: He walks past those waiting in the economy line and notices the looks and glares of other passengers as he walks up the business class queue. Often, people stop or cut in ahead of him. Derek assumes they think he is not supposed to be there. "I've had that numerous times, where it's like, 'Are you sure you are in the right place?' It's that reminder that 'you are travelling with us, but you are not one of us!'"

Travel Jolts, it seemed, are common; Grace Ononiwu, CBE, director of legal services at the Crown Prosecution Services, told me how she experienced UK customs on the way home from a business trip. She had travelled to East Africa to give a lecture. In East Africa, she was met from the plane by representatives of the Foreign Office and taken to a VIP room. She was taken to meet her personal bodyguard. She was taken to a hotel with an armed guard. She was treated like royalty. She was taken back to the airport in the capital. When she arrived at Birmingham Airport, she felt that security had "clocked her" as she wheeled her trolley to go through customs. They asked, "Madam, where have you come from?" She explained that she had travelled on business. She explained to the customs officer that she had travelled on behalf of the then director of Public Prosecutions. The colour drained from his face. He immediately closed her bag and told her she could go. That initial contact was solely because he had seen a black woman. Grace took his number and reported him. "It was important for him to reflect," she told me.

The effect of this kind of Jolt is that black leaders can feel they have to always be on alert when travelling alone. It goes without saying that they often have to be better dressed than their white colleagues. However, they also need a level of confidence and self-assurance to deal with these incidents. It is a reminder that, in the office and workspaces, they may have the luxury of being treated as an equal. However, once they leave that space, they are just another black person dealing with everyday racism. Many black leaders believe that it can be helpful for their white colleagues to understand this additional pressure that they face.

THE CLOSE COLLEAGUE JOLT

I remember the first day I arrived at my longest employment. I drove up through the woods and saw the most beautiful deer. I arrived at what looked like a cross between a historic English castle and a spectacular country house. I felt as if I had died and gone to heaven! For 17 years, I was on the faculty of an international business school. It was where I became a professor of practice. I considered myself to be very fortunate in that I thoroughly enjoyed and loved my work. I enjoyed the regular interactions with clients, participants and colleagues as we developed and delivered executive education interventions. This work involved me developing ideas with colleagues, discussing them with clients and working with participants in ways that truly make a difference to their lives inside and outside of work. Whilst in this employment, I took the opportunity to study for my doctorate and was supported by my manager to make this possible. Though it would be dishonest to pretend that my career has been idyllic, on the whole, the work was rewarding, so I chose to stay for many years.

I recall my boss sauntering into my office a couple of years after I had joined. The business school had won a significant piece of work with a global broadcaster – but they needed to demonstrate some diversity. So, although this was not my area of expertise, would I be interested in being on the team? I weighed up the risk of being the token black with the potential exposure and additional expertise I could gain through this experience. So, I decided to lean into the offer. So what if they needed me because I was a black face? If I could make it work for me, then I would go along with this. In any case, I had a lot of respect for my boss. He had been upfront with me, and I knew he meant well. Ten years later, I was again invited to an event at work because I was black – but this time, I was Jolted.

I had worked for many years alongside a colleague; let's call him Cameron. I considered him to be a good friend and a colleague. We often travelled together for work and got on well. I liked him. He invited me to accompany him to a meeting for a potential new client. I was quite pleased, as it was in a new business sector that I felt I could grow my experience. I also had a lot to offer, as I had a lot of experience with clients from this part of Europe. This could also be an opportunity to work alongside Cameron, with whom I worked well. I felt excitement at the prospect. The meeting was a relaxed, conversational affair. We worked hard to understand the clients' needs and made good progress during the meeting.

We left the client meeting and went on to have lunch in the business school staff dining room, where we sat with another colleague. "We've just been to a new client meeting," said Cameron. "I only brought Barbara because we needed a bit of diversity," he scoffed. I felt shocked and angry, in equal measure. The relationship with my colleague changed in an instant. He had pretended that I had been brought into the meeting as his equal. He then publicly diminished any sense of achievement I had felt in being part of the meeting. His tone was such that I remained silent for the entire lunch, unable to taste the food I was mechanically putting into my mouth – this provided time for me to take stock and SCAN.

I decided to challenge the colleague immediately. My comments did not come out quite right. I calmly and very slowly told him that I felt hurt by his comment. I was still angry, though. He was effusive in his apology and did not understand why he had hurt me. I did not want to offer a one-person training course on race. So, I left it there and gracefully accepted his apology.

Such incidents can cause long-term damage to the relationships that black leaders have with white colleagues. It can also lead black leaders to be reluctant to open up and form close bonds at work. A *Harvard Business Review* article[4] stresses the importance of black people opening up at work, as colleagues often feel they need to know you to work well with you. Yet, black people who have experienced such a Jolt can become even more reluctant to open up. They fear that they may reveal information that can be used against them. Organisations cannot pretend to be colour blind but need to constantly consider how to ensure that their leaders know how to behave in ways that have a positive impact on inclusion.

THE MISTAKEN IDENTITY JOLT

Amongst the black leaders I spoke to, many of them told me about mistaken identity Jolts. The moment where you are going about your business and suddenly you are confronted with a case of mistaken identity that reminds you of the stereotypes that others hold about the sorts of jobs you are allowed to do.

One of the leaders I interviewed works in recruitment. Let's call her Naomi. Naomi likes to dress well. She works with a personal stylist to ensure she gets her office look just right. All of her clothes are carefully picked out and matched with the right kinds of accessories. She loves the fact that she is often complimented on her clothing and her sense of style. In her line of work, everyone has to look smart – but she makes an extra effort. She works in central London and so tends to wear sneakers to and from the office. Her route to the office was always the same, through the sliding doors at the front of the building, up in the lift to her floor. Always uneventful. On this day, she walked through the door, showed her badge to the gentleman on the security desk and walked towards the lift. A woman was standing by the lift. The woman said to her at the lift door, "Are you the cleaner?" Naomi replied that she was not the cleaner. However, the lady asked her again, talking more slowly this time. Her tone was a mixture of impatience and disdain. This was not how Naomi was used to being addressed. She was also somewhat disgusted that this might be the way that black cleaners in her office were spoken to on a daily basis. The shock of this very public incident has stayed with her.

Another interviewee, Tony, told me about a meeting he had attended in Austria. It was with a colleague that he met with quite regularly and would typically wait in reception until called up. He went through the usual motions of signing in and waiting. When he got to his colleague's office, she had a joke for him., "Oh, one of my colleagues saw you come in downstairs and said, 'Oh, I see your drug dealer's arrived.'" Tony was shocked and embarrassed by the comment. It felt like an insult, a put-down.

My brother, Robert Beckford, a professor, had arrived in Canterbury in the south of England, where there were very few black people. He was there to take up a new post as a university professor. He would be the first black professor at this university. It was the first day of the month, and he found himself sitting in a large reception area with around ten other new joiners with whom he was to go through an induction process. As he was waiting in the reception area, he was approached by a tall gentleman in overalls. The man in the overalls asked Robert to follow him; it doesn't feel right, but Robert follows anyway – it's his first day, and he doesn't want to make a bad impression. Robert is led through to the kitchen! He initially thought he was being taken on a tour of the campus. Only when they asked him if he wanted to start work immediately was he seriously Jolted.

Robert did not respond at all. They had made an honest mistake. However, such mistakes never happened to white men in suits, he reminded me.

This kind of Jolt reminded me how the trauma of repeated racial incidents means that black people can be oversensitive in certain situations. I recall being asked by a co-worker in the dining room at the business school whether I could put her tray away. I was in the way, and she wanted to pass it to me. I responded rather sharply that I did not work in the kitchen. She said she knew that – she was just asking me to put her tray down so she would not have to lean over me!

Whilst most of the aforementioned cases were (hopefully) inadvertent, they probably betray some white people's biases about black people. They illustrate the preconceptions that some white people intuitively have about the roles that black people can do and where they belong. It may require an exhausting mental reach for some white people to imagine black people as senior executives in organisations. How though might this impact progression and promotion of black professionals? Research has shown that individuals with more white-sounding names receive 50 per cent more callbacks for interviews than those with black-sounding names.[5] US studies by Cunningham and Bopp,[6] and Carton and Rosette[7] showed that workplace racial stereotypes also mean that African Americans are evaluated negatively regardless of their performance and are seen as lacking the appropriate knowledge and skills for high-level positions.

THE "FAILED TO GET PROMOTION" JOLT

Selena had been working in science in the pharmaceutical industry for over 15 years. She has risen to the position of a senior research scientist within a global healthcare company. She decided that she was ready for a change that would increase the breadth of her experience. So, she applied to a new organisation. She felt that she was well suited for the job, possessing all the required experience and qualifications. There was a gruelling interview process. The initial interview went well, and she was invited back for a six-hour process involving a group of managers from across the organisation. At the end of the process, she was told that she had performed exceptionally well. "We think we can offer you the job, but before we make the formal offer, you need to speak to the head of the department who will sign it off. This is not meant to be a formal interview, but it's just for you to meet them before they sign the paperwork for the role." Selena met the head of the department, and the meeting went well. Then the company suddenly came back and said, "Sorry, you didn't get the role." It was all very confusing. She had made the application via a recruitment agency, so she pushed a little with them to see if she could understand what might have gone wrong at this critical moment. She reminded them that both they and the employer had said that this was a done deal. Eventually, the feedback came: "Oh, she didn't think that one of her key team members would look up to someone like you." Selena was shocked.

Was this about colour? She did not want to make that assumption. However, it was a team of all white people. Selena felt she knew what was meant by "the team wouldn't look up to me." However, in such a situation, there was nothing she could do. Selena did not tell anyone about this experience. She felt disappointment, anger and shame but kept all of that to herself.

Naomi also shared a story of a failed promotion Jolt. She had achieved all the targets needed to get the next promotion in the company. She was good at her job. One of the things that she had liked about recruitment was that it was a relatively transparent meritocracy. You reach your targets, and you get a bonus and/or you get a promotion. She had been working in risk and investment banking. It was a tough area, not only because it is competitive, but "because the candidates are very intelligent, they're mathematical, they've got PhDs. You can't sell to them, so you've got to approach them differently. That's why I'm good at what I'm doing because you learnt how to approach them."

Naomi's boss, Richard, had told her she would be sent on the appropriate leadership training course with three of her peers. She would become the first black leader at the new level. All the details of the training were circulated by email. Her peers received theirs, but Naomi did not. "Then, the other three people were in their training," she recalls. "I didn't get it. I sent my boss an email. 'What's happening?' I asked him. He ignored it. I emailed him again, and he ignored it again. I went over to his desk, and I said, 'Richard, where is my invitation to the training?' "

After several weeks, Richard eventually agreed to discuss it. In the meeting, he looked Naomi directly in the eye and said, "Naomi, I have no idea why you weren't on the training."

"You don't know why I'm not on the training with all the others?" I asked.

He said, "No, I don't know."

Was this about colour? Naomi felt powerless and deflated. She realised that there was nowhere to go with this conversation. "I think he thought I was going to say something, but I just thought, what is there to say?"

Greg, also a pseudonym, a technical specialist, had also experienced a couple of occasions where he had had to wait longer to get promotions than his white counterparts. On the one hand, he tried to pretend this was not happening yet. At another level, he accepted this as part of being a black man in a white workplace. He watched as his white colleagues, often with lower educational levels, progressed from below him to become his seniors. Was this race? Maybe he was simply not ready? However, one incident stands out for him. He was heading up the learning and development function within a manufacturing company. He got on well in the organisation and felt both respected and liked. He applied for a more senior position for which he was well qualified. He was surprised when the role was given to a white colleague with no knowledge of the function. He asked for feedback and was told, "You know, you don't really want to manage people" Greg was shocked because this was why he had applied for the role. "So, it was, kind of, a weird dynamic in terms of why I wasn't given the opportunity to do that role."

These kinds of Jolts can damage the confidence of black leaders. Racism is subtle, so how can you be certain that it was race? In the absence of clear, objective, unambiguous feedback, it becomes difficult for the black leader to understand what is actually happening. However, the statistics I offered in Chapter 1 illustrated the under-representation of black people at the top of organisations. This would suggest that there might be a broader systemic issue.

THE "THERE ISN'T A PROBLEM" JOLT

Jonathan Akwue of Publicis told me about a meeting he had been invited to near the beginning of his career in advertising. It was organised by the industry body that represents advertisers, the IPA. It was a real culture shock for him at the time on account of the lack of conversation about the need for diversity in the industry at that time. He had attended an ethnic diversity forum.

The guy who was chairing it at the time stood in front of a room of about 30 Black people, which was probably the entire Diverse workforce of advertising at the time. The guy stood there and said words to the effect of, "There really isn't a problem. We don't want to go down the American route of affirmative action," and all this. He was like, "We're British –" This was a Black guy, "– because we're British, that's not how we do things. It really isn't a problem, and I think we all just need to lighten up.

Jonathan was surprised to hear the head of the diversity forum deny the obvious. He had been one of the lucky few who had managed to have a successful career in advertising. Jonathan told me how he distinctly remembered standing outside these beautiful white-columned buildings in central London.

If I had a brick in my hand at that time, I would have thrown it through the window. Because I was like, this institution sits here, next to ambassador's residences and embassies in the heart of London. I was like, what world do you live in? You could walk into any advertising agency at the time. Not only would it be white, but it would be overwhelmingly middle class and over-whelmingly male, certainly at the top of those agencies. Something just snapped inside me. I remember it very distinctly.

For Jonathan, the Jolt caused him to make a conscious decision. He would ensure that he made a difference to inclusion and diversity in his industry.

This kind of Jolt, where clear evidence of racism is denied, and statistics are ignored, can cause deep hurt. When a person of colour is also putting forward this position, it can feel hypocritical. This reminded me of the feelings of shock, hurt and even betrayal that were expressed by many black leaders in the wake of the 2021 *Report of the Commission on Race and Ethnic Disparities*.[8] It is important that black leaders do not feel that racism is a figment of their imagination. Through their experience of Jolts, black leaders know that this is real. This reality needs to be accepted if real change is to happen.

The types of Jolts discussed in this chapter could be regarded as those of privileged black leaders. However, understanding these Jolts is an important starting point in having conversations around race that can help build inclusion. This is not to diminish other, often more traumatic events that can cause Jolts, like being stopped and roughed up by the police or being a victim of racist aggression.

In the examples discussed in this chapter, there are two kinds of responses to the Jolt. One is to ignore, withdraw and not comment as you are shocked into silence. The other is to calmly SCAN. There is, of course, a third response. This response is to directly react to the incident emotionally. This might involve becoming cross, angry or even abusive. This latter response might be equally understandable and legitimate. Faced with racism and injustice, individuals can feel hurt and show this in their response. It is interesting that those black leaders who have "made it" choose not to respond in that way.

Chapter 3 has identified the nature of everyday racist incidents and the considered response of black leaders. It has shown how black leaders succeed in spite of these Jolts. Section 2 strips away a further layer to explore how black leaders develop behavioural attributes that enable them to survive and thrive in this environment.

KEY TAKEAWAYS

- The Jolt is the moment when a racial incident or a comment shifts the unconscious sense of difference or being an outsider to the conscious.
- Jolts are common for black leaders both inside and outside the work environment.
- Recognising the Jolts is an essential step to understanding the instances of racism that black leaders experience.

QUESTIONS FOR REFLECTION

- How did you respond when reading about the Jolts in this chapter?
- Why do you think you responded in that way?
- How might you use your understanding of the Jolt in your relationship with your black colleagues?

NOTES

1 Bryant-Davis, T., & Ocampo, C. (2005). The Trauma of Racism. *The Counseling Psychologist* 33, 574–578.

2 Giller, E. (1999). What Is Psychological Trauma? *Sidran Institute.* www. sidran.org/resources/for-survivors-and-loved-ones/what-is-psychological-trauma/ [Last accessed 21 July 2021].

3 Sanchez-Hucles, B., & Jones, N. (2005).Breaking the Silence Around Race in Training, Practice, and Research. *The Counseling Psychologist* 33, 547–558.

4 Phillips, K. W. et al. (2018, March–April). Minorities Hesitate to Share Information about Themselves at Work: That's a Problem for Everyone. *Harvard Business Review.*

5 Bertrand, M., & Mullainathan, S. (2004). Are Emily and Greg More Employable Than Lakisha and Jamal? A Field Experiment on Labor Market Discrimination. *The American Economic Review* 94(4).

6 Cunningham, G., & Bopp, T. (2010). Race Ideology Perpetuated: Media Representations of Newly Hired Football Coaches. *Journal of Sports Media* 5(1).

7 Carton, A. M., & Rosette, A. S. (2011). Explaining Bias Against Black Leaders: Integrating Theory on Information Processing and Goal-Based Stereotyping. *Academy of Management Journal* 54(6), 1141–1158.

8 Commission on Race and Ethnic Disparities. (2021). *The Report of the Commission on Race and Ethnic Disparities.* www.gov.uk/government/publications/the-report-of-the-commission-on-race-and-ethnic-disparities/foreword-introduction-and-full-recommendations.

REFERENCES AND ADDITIONAL READING

Bertrand, M., & Mullainathan, S. (2004). Are Emily and Greg More Employable Than Lakisha and Jamal? A Field Experiment on Labor Market Discrimination. *The American Economic Review* 94(4).

Bryant-Davis, T., & Ocampo, C. (2005). The Trauma of Racism. *The Counseling Psychologist* 33, 574–578.

Carter, R. T. (2007). Racism and Psychological and Emotional Injury: Recognizing and Assessing Race-based Traumatic Stress. *The Counseling Psychologist* 35(1), 13–105.

Carton, A. M., & Rosette, A. S. (2011). Explaining Bias Against Black Leaders: Integrating Theory on Information Processing and Goal-based Stereotyping. *Academy of Management Journal* 54(6), 1141–1158.

Commission on Race and Ethnic Disparities. (2021). *The Report of the Commission on Race and Ethnic Disparities.* www.gov.uk/government/publications/the-report-of-the-commission-on-race-and-ethnic-disparities/foreword-introduction-and-full-recommendations

Cunningham, G., & Bopp, T. (2010). Race Ideology Perpetuated: Media Representations of Newly Hired Football Coaches. *Journal of Sports Media* 5(1).

Francois, S., & Davis, C. (2021). Lifting the Veil: Considering the Conceptualizations of Racism-based Trauma among Social Workers. *Qualitative Social Work* 1473325021997542.

Franklin, A. J., Boyd-Franklin, N., & Kelly, S. (2006). Racism and Invisibility: Race-related Stress, Emotional Abuse and Psychological Trauma for People of Color. *Journal of Emotional Abuse* 6(2–3), 9–30.

Giller, E. (1999). What Is Psychological Trauma? *Sidran Institute.* www.sidran.org/resources/for-survivors-and-loved-ones/what-is-psychological-trauma/ [Last accessed 21 July 2021].

Helms, J. E., Nicolas, G., & Green, C. E. (2010). Racism and Ethnoviolence as Trauma: Enhancing Professional Training. *Traumatology* 16(4), 53–62.

Kirkinis, K., Pieterse, A. L., Martin, C., Agiliga, A., & Brownell, A. (2021). Racism, Racial Discrimination, and Trauma: A Systematic Review of the Social Science Literature. *Ethnicity & Health* 26(3), 392–412.

Lowe, S. M., Okubo, Y., & Reilly, M. F. (2012). A Qualitative Inquiry into Racism, Trauma, and Coping: Implications for Supporting Victims of Racism. *Professional Psychology: Research and Practice* 43(3), 190.

Phillips, K. W., Rothbard, N. P., & Dumas, T. L. (2009). To Disclose or not to Disclose? Status Distance and Self-Disclosure in Diverse Environments. *Academy of Management Review* 34(4), 710–732.

Phillips, K. W. et al. (2018, March–April). Minorities Hesitate to Share Information about Themselves at Work: That's a Problem for Everyone. *Harvard Business Review.*

Sanchez-Hucles, B., & Jones, N. (2005). Breaking the Silence Around Race in Training, Practice, and Research. *The Counseling Psychologist* 33, 547–558.

Sanchez-Hucles, J. V. (1999). Racism: Emotional Abusiveness and Psychological Trauma for Ethnic Minorities. *Journal of Emotional Abuse* 1(2), 69–87.

Yoshino, K., & Smith, C. (2014). Fear of Being Different Stifles Talent. *Harvard Business Review* 92(3), 27–28.

SECTION 2

HOW WE GET ON:
THE MODEL BLACK

"YOU FIT IN WELL HERE"
The Model Black

This chapter

- *introduces the profile black British leaders adopt to succeed: the Model Black,*
- *identifies the nine attributes common to black British leaders in organisations in Britain,*
- *explains how being the Model Black affects the health of black leaders and*
- *considers how racial tropes in broader society contribute to the requirement for Model Black behaviours.*

For those of us who are perceived to be successful, there's an element where increasingly you get confident in your own skin, literally, in whatever, and the value that that brings. The earlier you get that in the organization, the better.

Anon, Senior Executive, Financial Services

Trouble is, I ain't jumping in no trench. That's what my ancestors did. They did that so I could stand on their shoulders. They didn't want me to jump in the same trench as them. I'm supposed to be taking their learning and standing on their shoulders and sitting around that table where strategy is developed that impacts everybody.

Grace Ononiwu, CBE, Director of Legal
Services, Crown Prosecution Service (CPS)

DOI: 10.4324/9781003200482-8

If you joined the Black employment group, great, be a part of that network, but that network isn't going to get you to the C-suite.

Anon, Senior Executive, Technology

That network of people, colleagues and friends that are from your network, your cultural identity, again, it's really important so you don't feel lonely so that you can have those conversations that maintain your emotional resilience.

Patricia Miller, OBE, Chief Executive, NHS

I have good sponsors in my line of career. Interestingly enough, the sponsors I've had have not been black. It's also important to highlight that.

Paul Aliu, Head of Global Governance,
Chief Medical Office, Novartis

In all of these circumstances, in order to feel comfortable yourself, and also make other people feel comfortable around you, you have to learn the second language, literally, in some cases. . . . I think for some people, it can carry a kind of erosion of the soul because you can get to a place where you sort of don't quite know who you are.

Sir Trevor Phillips, CBE former head of the
Commission for Racial Equality

Are there particular attributes that successful black leaders possess? Are there certain characteristics that they have in common that enable them to successfully navigate their white workplaces? To address this question, I spoke to 28 senior leaders,[1] most of whom had over 20 years of experience in corporate life in a variety of organisations. I also spoke with David Lammy, MP, and Sir Trevor Philips, CBE, former head of the Equalities and Human Rights Commission. To gain the perspectives of younger leaders, I additionally interviewed six young professionals with an average of four years in their professions to understand how they are experiencing race at work. Their experiences are discussed in Chapter 10. This was a small-scale qualitative study that relied on non-probability sampling. Through my own contacts and a few "cold calls" via LinkedIn, I spoke with individuals who were prepared to be open and candid. Some were prepared to be named, and some were not. Participants came from a range of organisations, including professional services companies, manufacturing, the NHS and the police force. These senior and experienced leaders were mostly aged between 40 and 60. The vast majority were in the top 5 per cent of UK taxpayers. I used a semi-structured interview to elicit information on their personal histories and workplace experiences.

Out of these conversations emerged characteristics that formed the profile of the Model Black (Figure 4.1).

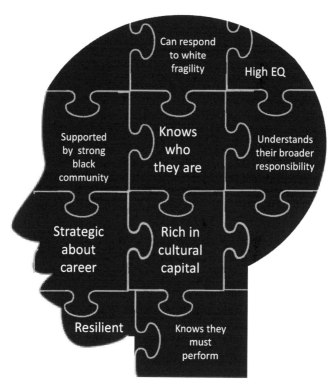

Figure 4.1 The attributes of the Model Black

THE PROFILE OF THE MODEL BLACK

I take for granted that the Model Black possesses all the fundamental technical and interpersonal skills required to be effective in their role. This is an entry-level requirement. The characteristics below are what this research suggests provides them with the X factor to succeed. This research showed that the Model Black. . .

. . . knows who they are

It can be difficult for black children to grow up in Britain and develop a positive identity and a positive sense of self. However, this was something that the Model Black leaders possessed. Many of the Aspirers and Drivers, identified in Chapter 2, spoke about pivotal moments in the development of their identities. Patricia Miller, OBE, chief executive of Dorset County Hospital Foundation Trust, talked about a time when she was 17. She recalls a long visit to Barbados that had the biggest influence on how she saw herself than anything else that happened in her life. Metropolitan Police Superintendent Robyn Williams talked about a programme that she attended with Len Garrison in Nottingham. She recalled a course at the African Caribbean Family and Friends Center where she was introduced to pan-Africanism and African Caribbean history. The course transformed her: "It changed the way that I walk. It lifted my self-esteem. It opened me up to a history that I had never been shown or understood. It was empowering, illuminating, exciting."

David Lammy, MP, referred to the sense of empowerment he gained from his time amongst successful blacks in the US. This exposure, knowing your history, understanding where you are from and standing tall in this knowledge was evident in half of the black leaders interviewed. They understood that entering the workplace without a clear sense of who you are can lead to a feeling of dislocation: You do not feel confident in who you are and are then criticised on account of your difference. There was also a view that when you are confident about your identity, you are both able to recognise acts of racism and able to deal with them in a mature way – knowing who you are meant that when you experience racism, you are more likely to understand the broader context of racism. You understand why it occurs and how it persists and are therefore more inclined to "go high." This challenge of identity seemed to be less of an issue for the Risers and Deservers referred to in Chapter 2. They were clear in their background and history. Their sense of self had been developed through being in the racial majority during their schooling. They felt they were equally affected by discrimination in the UK but were more inclined to believe that this was something that they could power through. They could succeed regardless of any racism they might encounter.

... has cultural capital

I recently joined a call with a white facilitator with whom I was going to be working on a global programme. He talked about where he lived, and I showed some interest by mentioning that some of my family lived close to his town. He talked about the area, explaining that this town was very close to where he used to keep his horses. He also added that there was a fabulous golf course nearby, which, unfortunately, he was no longer able to use as often as he wanted. I have zero interest in horses or golf. However, I entered into a conversation with him around all things equine. I happened to have spent a month learning to ride (or rather falling from the horse!) during my teenage stay with a family in Germany.

Many of the black leaders I spoke to felt no desire to learn to ride, ski, play golf or rugby. However, they emphasised the importance of being able to have some knowledge of the interests of the dominant culture in their part of the organisation. As I mentioned in Chapter 2, Bourdieu[2] developed the idea of cultural capital as resources that contribute towards upward social mobility. He had in mind things like knowledge, skills and education. In this context, there is a particular focus on the things that matter within organisations that enable individuals to be accepted and promoted – having an interest in areas enables you to connect with others and then consequently feel part of the "in crowd." The Model Black profile suggests that, at minimum, you should have the conversational skills that enable you to demonstrate a deep sense of curiosity and interest. Black leaders recognised that this willingness to engage with interest increased their "fit" score and therefore potentially enhanced their career prospects.

This area of cultural capital is difficult to write about because whilst leaders talked about the importance of understanding areas that were interesting to the dominant, often white male middle-class culture, there was also a real sense of the importance of keeping one's own identity and not becoming something that was too far from who you really were. However, the advice was certainly that, even when others showed no interest in things that were important to you – if you were serious about getting on, you would need to ignore their disinterest in you and focus on getting yourself educated in what matters to them.

... knows how to respond to white fragility

In her book, *White Fragility*, DiAngelo[3] explains that when their world views are challenged, white people can feel that this represents a challenge to their identities as good, moral people. DiAngelo explains how even suggesting that being white has meaning can trigger emotions like anger and fear and can cause argumentation or withdrawal from a stress-inducing situation. The result is discomfort and anxiety. These responses on the part of white people rebuff any challenges and allow white people to return to their racial comfort.

Once the area of race becomes the subject of discussion, the response from white people is often anger, silence or disbelief. The response from the black people in this study is often hurt, anger and exasperation. As the non-dominant culture, black people often have daily negative experiences, such as the Jolts discussed in Chapter 3, which inform the way that they see the world. White people may not have these experiences. When black people are challenged or come up against white fragility, they need to have a repertoire of responses dictated by the SCAN (Chapter 1). The typical responses of the Model Black include the following:

- Take a deep breath and **feign curiosity**. Ask them to tell you more. Inquire into how they came to think that way before offering any response.
- Take a deep breath and offer an **educational resource**. One leader told how she often responded with, "Have you read such and such book; you really ought to take a look at. . . ."

- Try to talk about your experience in an **objective manner**, as if you are talking about another person, which can distance you from the situation.
- Use a **"velvet fist"** approach, carefully choosing language to ensure white colleagues are not alienated.
- **Ignore** – but do not hold it against your white colleagues.

The black leaders interviewed for this book stressed the importance of assuming positive intent, regardless of how they chose to respond.

. . . is part of a strong, reliable black community

Whether it is to share the successes of a promotion or a business deal or talk about some of the daily experiences and trauma of being black – you need to be able to share it with people who understand your experience. One leader told me of the stress of having her daily experiences invalidated by her white husband each evening. It is important to have individuals who truly "get it," with whom you can process your feelings. Some found this a useful way to diffuse any anger they felt before it emerged in the workplace.

The concept of black affinity groups in the workplace was less common for those who had spent their careers in British and European organisations than for those working in organisations with a strong US origin or base. Derek Bruce, an HR professional, told me, "We've never spoken about the mental stress, about the pressure, about the need to achieve, about the pressure from parents to always succeed, the questioning. We don't talk about it, and because it's being held in and not spoken about for so long, we professionals do burnout." Black networks provide an important space for sharing experiences and having them validated. As Patricia Miller put it, "We all go through that moment of did that really just happen? Did they really mean that the way they said it? You've got those individuals to go back to and have that conversation to realise that you're not going mad actually, that the thing you think you saw or you heard or you felt or experienced was real, so that that you can then go back and challenge that, even if it's afterwards." There was the added benefit of being part of a group that can collectively raise grievances, as well as bring suggestions to improve inclusion.

Many black leaders who had spent much of their careers in large corporates mentioned that they had gone through their careers almost entirely without talking to a black person at work about their problems. This had taken a toll on their well-being. This unwillingness to talk about problems may be a generational issue that I will unpack further in Chapter 10. The experience of not talking about race was more evident among individuals in the private sector. Within the public sector, there was a longer history of black networks and associations.

... is strategic about their career

The Model Black knows that as part of a minority that is often negatively perceived, strategic career planning is essential. This was about long-term planning, effective networking and being proactive in terms of career progression. Some of the black leaders felt that they had felt grateful to have a good job, and this had sadly stifled some of their early ambition. They stressed the importance of having a proactive approach to personal development and promotion. These are not things that should be left to chance; they should be thought through and clear strategies and objectives and timescales laid out. Even if ultimately the goals were not achieved, the plan was important. A six-year US study by Thomas and Gabarro[4] supports both the necessity of strategic career planning for people of colour and the need to demonstrate more competence than their white colleagues.

The importance of having a mentor to support their career planning could not be overstressed. As black people often lack connections within industries and organisations, the role of a mentor in helping them to navigate their organisation was critical. The leaders had mentors within and outside the organisation. These mentors did not have to be black, but the benefits of at least one mentor with an understanding of the sensitivities of being a minority was emphasised. The black leaders recognised that some other minority groups might have this support in their communities. However, this was seldom the case for the black community.

Networking was also critical to career development. I recall joining Boots Pharmaceuticals as a young graduate and being introduced to what was known as "the Progress Club." This was a networking group to which you had to be "introduced" by another member. It met several times a year, and it was a great opportunity to meet with senior leadership within the organisation and others who were "marked for success." As a black person, it can be harder to build your network. Networks are often built outside the organisation in social settings from which black people can feel excluded. However, as much effort as this might take, black leaders, recognised the importance of identifying individuals within the organisation who could be supporters for their career progression.

Moving around different organisations was also seen as essential. I spoke to a senior leader who had spent some of his career in the US. He commented that he saw lots of good black people in his UK organisation, but there was never going to be space for them all to get promoted to a senior level. He noticed that these leaders stayed and complained rather than looked outside for other opportunities. He questioned why this was. He had learnt early on that there was little benefit in being loyal to an organisation. What was also stressed was the importance of finding a workplace with a culture in which you can thrive.

Seeing beyond the work that you are currently doing was also important. One leader told me how he was invited to sit on an internal cross-functional committee many years ago. He had a senior research role and knew that being on this committee was "donkey work." He had a white mentor who told him that nobody really wants to do this role because they cannot see beyond the actual work: "You don't need to do that role to show that you can do it, but I feel you need to do that role to give you the right exposure to certain people to know what you're able to do." He did the boring work, and it raised his profile immensely.

Requesting a sponsor was mentioned by two individuals. There was a benefit in having someone to guide your progression through the organisation. This was seen as a more recent US phenomenon. Leaders talked more about accidentally having someone in their department or business area who liked them and looked out for them.

. . . is emotionally intelligent

Being black in the workplace means that you may have to make more effort to read the room. You need to make more effort to understand others and get along with people. You also become acutely aware that there are parts of yourself that are not welcome in the work environment. You need to work out how to behave so that others feel comfortable around you. In many of the leaders, this manifested itself as a deep level of self-awareness. This was about having emotional intelligence (EQ).[5] None of the black leaders I spoke with used the term emotional intelligence; however, it was evident in the way they spoke about their leadership style. EQ is an attribute that is as essential as intelligence (IQ) in the workplace. Research has demonstrated that emotional intelligence is a critical leadership capability. It differentiates average from outstanding performers. According to Goleman, it is the process whereby an individual can control their behaviour to maintain and develop day-to-day relationships with others effectively.

I observed a heightened sensitivity in the leaders' ability to recognise the effect of their behaviour on those around them and be able to modulate it accordingly. The black leaders also possessed a lot of empathy; they showed a sincere understanding of how their white counterparts saw the world. One female leader told me how she spent two evenings considering her response to the Black Lives Matter events before writing an internal note to her colleagues. Her concern was how it would make them feel if she expressed her emotions around the issue. Another recognised how hard it must be for her colleagues to treat her as "one of them" when she was probably the only black person they had ever encountered. All black leaders talked about the sensitivity they had learnt to show when working in an atmosphere infused with microaggressions and white fragility. Many of the leaders knew of black colleagues who had "failed" because they lacked this sensitivity. I return to the notion of EQ in Chapter 7, where I discuss how the black men I interviewed were particularly strong in this attribute.

. . . understands their broader responsibility

Successful black leaders are often asked to get involved in work to help the organisation progress its EDI agenda. Even though this work is actual labour, they do it willingly. This might involve being part of certain committees, helping with community work and the recruitment of other black employees. All this takes time and effort.

The Model Black knows that there may be no extra thanks for this work. They see the importance of being patient as they wait for the organisation to catch up with their thinking and expectations regarding being compensated for their efforts. Many leaders talked about challenging their organisations to give them credit for this work.

Black leaders recognised they had a responsibility to other black people within the workplace and within the broader society. This means that it is essential to give something back to the community. Having taken time to understand organisational cultures and having successfully navigated them, they saw it as their duty to pass this knowledge on to the next generation. Many had become mentors. Derek Bruce, a senior HR professional, had set up a mentoring association matching black leaders from a range of countries and sectors. Over half of the leaders were actively involved in mentoring or other work within black communities.

Within their organisation, some black leaders confessed that they could not be seen to promote others of colour. Sometimes, there was anxiety that you would be seen to be doing favours to an individual, even if they are the best person for the job. Research has identified this phenomenon in senior female leaders,[6] who, once they have "arrived," often want to be the only woman with a seat at the table. Black leaders cautioned their black colleagues not to emulate this.

. . . accepts they have to perform better to be equal

To succeed, black leaders have to be outstanding in their work, performing at a standard above that expected from their white counterparts. All black people are familiar with the phrase that you must be twice as good to get half as far. From a very young age, you are told about being better to be equal. It is the chant of the black migrant who wants to succeed in a white foreign land. The black leaders said that this was so much a given that they would not have raised it in conversation with me; Grace Ononiwu, CBE director of legal services at the Crown Prosecution Service, told me how she was over-qualified each time she applied for a role. Naomi, who works in recruitment, talked about always having to exceed her targets. Leaders talked of knowing that they would never be able to drop the ball and get away with it. As someone who was different, the spotlight was on you. There was always a sense that you had to continuously prove yourself. For many, this resulted in huge personal pressure and even illness.

... needs to be resilient

The Model Black recognises that they live in a society where people have biases, and some people are out and out racist. They do not expect them to go away. They learn to live with them and find ways of staying resilient. There was a sense that those black colleagues who were not sufficiently resilient simply did not make it to the top. Naomi, a recruitment consultant, told me how suppressing so much on a day-to-day basis meant that you had to be resilient. She had a personal coach and a nutritionist in addition to her network of friends. Robyn Williams, a Metropolitan Police superintendent, told me about her "green juice." This was an actual drink she made each day, but it was also a metaphor for the importance of black people to stay resilient. One leader said that being constantly on guard was taking a toll on her health. She had recognised the importance of good nutrition early in her career. Black leaders also talked about staying resilient by very consciously compartmentalising their home and work lives.

The Model Black leaders interviewed for this book stressed the importance of black professionals making conscious choices about how they want to be in the workplace. Knowing the implications of those choices is critical. They understood and accepted that being black often meant that you carried a significant burden. This burden was heavier for some leaders than others. They stressed the importance of younger black professionals recognising the toll that it may take on them to be the Model Black. Each individual needed to make a conscious choice about the extent to which they feel able to do the things necessary to "fit" and be successful at work. The physical toll that goes with the profile of the Model Black could be described as weathering.

"WEATHERING" AND THE MODEL BLACK

Black leaders recognise that they need to be selective about the parts of themselves that they bring to work. They feel that they cannot bring as much of themselves into the work environment as many of their white colleagues. They have norms, values and behaviours of which they are proud, but they often feel the need to keep parts of themselves hidden.

The Model Black recognises the work involved in preventing themselves from falling into traps around stereotypes. They know that this takes work. Model Black leaders talk about having to go to work with their brains running, trying to process "all this stuff" and stay one step ahead.

The experiences of black leaders in being on the receiving end of overt and subtle racism and of navigating their white workspaces can, over time, have a detrimental effect on the physical and mental health of black workers in the organisations, a concept referred to as "weathering." The idea of weathering was first identified in 1992 by Dr Arline Geronimus[7] as a possible explanation for maternal and infant health disparities between black and white women. The weathering hypothesis posited that black people experience earlier health deterioration than white people as a consequence of the cumulative impact of repeated experience with social or economic adversity and political marginalisation.[8] However, in a 2006[9] study, Geronimus and her colleagues identified evidence that racial inequalities in health could NOT be explained by racial differences in poverty. There had to be another explanation for black bodies ageing at a faster rate than their chronological age in a way that is not seen in their white counterparts. The suggestion was, therefore, that this ageing could be a result of the daily psychological stresses of being black. Prof David Williams[10] at Harvard University and colleagues have presented evidence supporting the idea that black people experience greater psychological wear and tear and are ageing faster than their white counterparts on account of the racism they face.

Black leaders in the workplace are often subject to treatment and comments that are not faced by their white counterparts. Additionally, they have to SCAN and are often overly conscious of the impression they are making. The culmination of this treatment and their behaviour may contribute to weathering – black people become tired; they get ill. Although they recognise that this is not on account of any intentional bad behaviour or ill will from their colleagues, the leaders interviewed for this book talked about having to put on an additional layer of armour each day, having to be extra resilient. The analogy of preparing to run a marathon was used on more than one occasion. In the same way, as they would prepare for a marathon with lots of physical and psychological preparation, they prepared to deal with the types of behaviour that were not an issue for their white co-workers. There was also a sense that the course of the marathon was precarious – as a black person, colleagues and the organisation could turn against you in sudden and unexpected ways.

RACIAL TROPES AND THE MODEL BLACK LEADER

The Model Black Leader exists, in part, in response to the existing tropes concerning black people in the British workplace and society. These tropes can cause unintentional racist behaviour.

Why is it that colleagues who would deny that they have a racist bone in their body inadvertently respond to black people in ways that black people experience as racist? Some of the explanation for this lies in the discourse around black people in Britain. History has influenced the images and discourse around what being black means, and this narrative has impacted perceptions around colour that cause bias and negative actions towards black people. An understanding of where these ideas come from can help explain racist behaviour. This knowledge also reveals why certain behaviours may seem minor to the person who is racialised as white, but they may represent part of a bigger picture in a broader historical context for the black person on the receiving side. I explore four of these tropes.

Apprehension around the black male body

Terry is the new senior recruit at a finance consultancy. He is the only black man on the team and the only senior black manager in his office block in the City. Every day, he comes in through the main doors, shows his pass to security. He then waits for an appropriate lift. Terry is now at week seven, and I would expect that most people have seen him around. So, why is it that, every time he enters the lift, he notices people physically moving away from him and can sense that the women are holding their handbags that bit tighter when he is there?

The black male body can evoke anxiety and apprehension in the workplace. Where does this apprehension arise from, and why should that matter in the workplace? The idea that there are three races – Caucasian, Negroid and Mongoloid – emerged in Germany in the late 18th century. Blumenbach, a German anthropologist, classified the races by skin pigmentation and skull size.[11] There was a clear racial hierarchy, with the Caucasians representing the most superior and the most beautiful race. Such ideas around racial categorisation, together with other early work in anthropology, spread and formed the basis of race-based policies that lasted into the late 19th and mid-to-late 20th centuries. These policies were used to justify political actions such as segregation, immigration restrictions as well as viewpoints that were based on prejudice.

The idea that the black male body was something to be feared was also reinforced during the Enlightenment through the work of Edward Long, an English-born British slave owner, in his highly controversial work, *The History of Jamaica*,[12] first published in 1774. These racist views were common among other writers at that time, including David Hume[13] and Immanuel Kant.[14] In these writings, the black male body was regarded as uncivilised and brutish. The black man was seen as something that could cause harm, and the black male body was seen as violent and animalistic. Their racist views became commonplace among other writers who relied on accounts from slave masters and missionaries for their descriptions of black people. These ideas have permeated the images and discourse around black people over the centuries. Over time we have internalised these ideas because of the things we have heard and the images we have observed. Consequently, these ideologies shape our thinking whether we like it or not. Foucault[15] talks about the notion of the discursive formation, the idea that societies possess the kinds of discourses that they accept to be true to sustain a "regime of truth." This desire to sustain this image of the scary black man can be seen in 20th- and 21st-century films and press coverage.

As black men rise to higher levels in organisations, the idea that they are to be feared remains a continuing association. This association may exist at a subconscious level, but it continues to be played out in workplace behaviours, as told by a senior leader:

> In some cases where people are having a meeting with me. . . . They are planning to come and have a meeting with me where I'm the decision-maker, and they're totally unprepared to come

and have that discussion with a black man. I've seen faces flicker from shock to surprise — "Are you sure you're the one that should be here?" They get very flustered. Earlier on, I got a little bothered about it; now, I've evolved to diffuse it. "Surprise!" I'll say, "You're meeting a black man! Let's get started."

Whilst negative associations with the black male body may persist, there is also another trope that young early career black professionals talk about: the notion of a certain type of black professional man associated with being "cool." This will be discussed further in Chapter 10.

The black female as obedient carer

"I come into the room, and I can see what's happening. There are drinks laid out, and nobody has as yet served the coffee. There are white women there as well. I decided privately that I was not going to go and pour the drinks. Then the Director asks me, 'would you mind. . . ?'"

"In our firm, I notice that the black female trainees are always expected to do the 'grunt work.' They are not asked to do the more creative strategic thinking that it's often offered to their white counterparts, rather the tasks that require their narrower legal skills."

Whereas history has caused black men to be defined as violent brutes, attitudes around black women leaders at work have their place in other tropes. One of those is that of the "mammy."[16] The mammy emanates from the period of slavery when black women were taken away from their own families to nurture and care for white families. These black women often put the needs of others above their own. This notion of the black woman as the nurturing, motherly self-sacrificing individual still plays a role in the way black leaders are perceived in the workplace today.[17] Like many other images from slavery, the image of the mammy represents a controlling ideology. It is about keeping black women in their place. So, black women are often expected to carry out the helper role. What this means is that when the black woman steps outside this role and decides to be more assertive, this is difficult for others to tolerate. Hence, the perception that she is aggressive. This perceived aggression is likely to be the manifestation of her deciding not to take on the role of the mammy. So, she instead becomes the "angry black woman," a notion I expand on in Chapter 7.

This matters for black female leaders and organisations because sitting at the intersection of gender and race, black women do not want to be called upon to do the serving and nurturing role. Equally, they do not want to be denied the opportunity to speak up for fear of being labelled as aggressive or angry. A black leader told me how she could never assert herself without being criticised, whereas the same or even more forceful behaviour was accepted in their white female colleagues:

> There was a white woman, a managing director of one of the regions. She was swearing, effing, and blinding, telling all sorts. The CEO rang her afterwards and said, "Sometimes I just enjoy us having a challenging conversation." A black woman would never keep her job if that happened.

So she would never contemplate behaving in that way.

The black leader as unintelligent and lazy

One of the senior leaders, who we will call Carl, told me how he found out that his boss, an inspector in the police force, had gone through his written report and attempted to grammatically correct it. "I had the sense that the Inspector thought that, because I was not white, he was trying to prove that I could not speak English. At the time, it felt he was deliberately trying to undermine me." Carl experienced a lot of direct criticism when he was promoted above his white colleagues. "People would double-check what you had told them. There would be people that were openly hostile, and their body language basically said, 'I'm not listening. I don't value you. I don't respect you.'"

Selena, a senior technologist, told me how she was in a role where she and a white colleague were due to be promoted to a senior managerial level. Her white colleague got the promotion immediately:

> I really had to fight for mine, and that was six months after she got promoted whereas previously, we had the same experience,

and they should have promoted both of us at the same time. I had to make additional efforts to demonstrate my ability. Eventually, I did get it, but I always wondered why she got hers so readily when I had to really justify mine.

Why is the ability of black people often not trusted? Why is it that black leaders often take longer to get promoted than their white colleagues? This may be linked to the idea that black people are intrinsically less intelligent than white people and consequently not suited for senior leadership roles. Part of the Enlightenment, David Hume[18] puts forward the view that black people were naturally inferior to whites. The idea was that there were inborn intellectual differences between Europeans and Africans. This latter concept was a key tenet of plantocracy racism which was driven by the need to justify the enslavement of Africans to drive wealth and profit for plantation owners. In plantocracy racism, the idea that Africans were lazy also legitimised slave owners in working black people harder. The thinking around different races having different IQs was popularised more recently in the *Bell Curve*,[19] suggesting that there is a black-white IQ gap. I do **not** purport that white colleagues are reading such controversial texts and are using them to judge the ability of their black colleagues. The reminder is that these ideas have influenced the way black people are viewed in society and so necessarily influence the way black people are viewed in leadership roles.

The black female as sexually available

One black leader told me about an organisation she worked in where the white men kept a book that recorded the sexual attractiveness of the women they worked with. Each kind of woman was given a score based on their sexual desirability. Black women were given by far the highest ratings. Points were awarded to the men when they successfully bedded any of the women in question. This resulted in black women joining the organisation, not recognising why they were being so avidly courted by their white male colleagues, only to be dropped once the relationship had served its point-scoring purpose. As a consequence, the black women in the company were treated longingly by white men and shown hostility by white women. This hostility was due in part to the black women's apparent advantage in possessing age-defying skin! Another senior black leader told me how the men she met were "overly familiar" with her in a way that they never were with her white female colleagues. On one occasion, a client invited her to his home for a "cooking" session. He was persistent – she refused.

These examples support the notion of the black woman as sexually available. Patricia Hill-Collins talks about the Jezebel[20] (the sexually aggressive black woman) as a controlling image in the oppression of blacks. The image has its roots in slavery and provides a rationale that justified the sexual assaults by white men on black women. Like the US "welfare mother," it has become a socially constructed weapon that enabled the subordination of black women. A US leader once told me how a white politician had come to speak at her company. At the time, she was eight months pregnant. The politician walked around the room, stood next to her and decided to rub his hand on her pregnant belly. He wandered around the room, came back and rubbed her tummy a second time. None of the UK leaders had such a brazen example of public overfamiliarity; however, amongst the two who spoke out, there was a sense of feeling a sense of physical and sexual unease around their male colleagues. They did not know how much of this was about gender and how much was about race.

It is interesting that in this study, the issue of female sexuality was raised only twice. I have also heard it talked about among black professionals. Was this simply a rare occurrence? Maybe it was simply not an issue in this sample? Or perhaps this was a topic that felt too uncomfortable, embarrassing or distasteful to raise with me?

MODEL BLACK BEHAVIOURS: A RESPONSE TO THE TROPES

There is more to the Model Black than the elements of the profile discussed previously. This research identified three ways of behaving that are critical for success. The following chapters will describe the three behaviours of the Model Black. These behaviours are employed to effectively navigate their work environment. Black leaders need to be more like their middle-class white colleagues and hide parts of their black selves, this is squaring. Black leaders learn over time when it is appropriate to talk about the challenges and injustices they face as black leaders. This is the behaviour of self-silencing. Black leaders understand how to minimise and play down parts of their style to make their white colleagues more comfortable; this is softening. The following chapters discuss how each of these strategies plays out for black British leaders and examine the implications for the Model Black, their colleagues and inclusion more generally.

KEY TAKEAWAYS

- The research among 30 leaders identified nine key characteristics that successful black leaders recognised as important factors in achieving success in their workplaces
- Being the Model Black is accepted by black leaders as an essential part of their route to success
- The risk of "weathering" exists for black leaders as they achieve success
- The model black behaviours represent a response to the broader societal racial tropes that impact how black leaders are viewed and treated in the workplace

---

QUESTIONS FOR REFLECTION

- What are your thoughts on the characteristics of the Model Black?
- How aware are you of the kinds of efforts made by black leaders in your organisation?
- To what extent do you recognise the impact of tropes in your attitude to black colleagues?
- What are your success characteristics, and how do they differ from what you have read here?

NOTES

1 There was one US citizen amongst the interviewees.
2 Bourdieu, P. (1986). The Forms of Capital. In J. G. Richardson (Ed.), *Handbook of Theory and Research for the Sociology of Education* (pp. 241–258). New York: Greenwood Press.
3 DiAngelo, R. (2019). *White Fragility*. UK: Penguin Books Ltd.

4 Thomas, D. A., & Gabarro, J. J. (1999). *Breaking Through: The Making of Minority Executives in Corporate America*. Boston, MA: Harvard Business Review Press.

5 Goleman, D. (2004). *Emotional Intelligence: Why It Can Matter More Than IQ & Working with Emotional Intelligence*. London: Bloomsbury.

6 Staines, G., Tavris, C., & Jayaratne, T. E. (1974). The Queen Bee Syndrome. *Psychology Today* 7, 55–60; Sobczak, A. (2018). The Queen Bee Syndrome. The Paradox of Women Discrimination on the Labour Market. *Journal of Gender and Power* 51(1).

7 Geronimus, A. T. (1992). The Weathering Hypothesis and the Health of African-American Women and Infants: Evidence and Speculations. *Ethnicity & Disease* 2(3), 207–221.

8 Geronimus, A. T. (1996). Black/White Differences in the Relationship of Maternal Age to Birthweight: A Population-Based Test of the Weathering Hypothesis. *Social Science & Medicine* 42(4), 589–597.

9 Geronimus, A. T., Hicken, M., Keene, D., & Bound, J. (2006). "Weathering" and Age Patterns of Allostatic Load Scores Among Blacks and Whites in the United States. *American Journal of Public Health* 96(5), 826–833. https://doi.org/10.2105/AJPH.2004.060749.

10 Williams, D. R., et al. (2019). Racism and Health: Evidence and Needed Research. *Annual Review of Public Health* 40(1), 105–125.

11 Painter, N. I. (2010). *The History of White People*. New York: W.W. Norton.

12 Long, E. (2002). *The History of Jamaica: Reflections on Its Situation, Settlements, Inhabitants, Climate, Products, Commerce, Laws and Government*. Montreal: McGill-Queen's University Press.

13 Coventry, A. M., & Valls, A. (eds), (2018). *David Hume on Morals, Politics, and Society*. New Haven and London: Yale University Press.

14 Kleingeld, P. (2007). Kant's Second Thoughts on Race. *The Philosophical Quarterly* 57, 573–592.

15 Foucault, M., & Sheridan, A. (1977). *Discipline and Punish: The Birth of the Prison*. London: Allen Lane.

16 Collins, P. H. (1991). Controlling Images and Black Women's Oppression. *Seeing Ourselves: Classic, Contemporary, and Cross-Cultural Readings in Sociology* 4, 266–273.

17 Bell, E. L., & Nkomo, S. M. (2001). *Our Separate Ways: Black and White Women and the Struggle for Professional Identity*. Boston: Harvard Business School Press.

18 Hume et al., *David Hume on Morals, Politics, and Society*.

19 Murray, C., & Herrnstein, R. J. (1996). *The Bell Curve: Intelligence and Class Structure in American Life*. New York: Simon and Schuster University of North Carolina Press.

20 Collins, P. H. (1991). Controlling Images and Black Women's Oppression. *Seeing Ourselves: Classic, Contemporary, and Cross-Cultural Readings in Sociology* 4, 266–273.

REFERENCES AND ADDITIONAL READING

Bell, E. L., & Nkomo, S. M. (2001). *Our Separate Ways: Black and White Women and the Struggle for Professional Identity*. Boston: Harvard Business School Press.

Bourdieu, P. (1986). The Forms of Capital. In J. G. Richardson (Ed.), *Handbook of Theory and Research for the Sociology of Education* (pp. 241–258). New York: Greenwood Press.

Carter, R. T. (2007). Racism and Psychological Emotional Injury: Recognizing and Assessing Race-based Traumatic Stress. *Counseling Psychologist* 35, 13–105. https://doi.org/10.1177/0011000006292033

Chapple, R. L., Jacinto, G. A., Harris-Jackson, T. N., & Vance, M. (2017). Do# BlackLivesMatter? Implicit Bias, Institutional Racism and Fear of the Black Body. *Ralph Bunche Journal of Public Affairs* 6(1), 2.

Collins, P. H. (1991). Controlling Images and Black Women's Oppression. *Seeing Ourselves: Classic, Contemporary, and Cross-Cultural Readings in Sociology* 4, 266–273.

Collins, P. H. (2000). *Black Feminist Thought: Knowledge, Consciousness, and the Politics of Empowerment*. London and New York: Routledge.

Coventry, A. M., & Valls, A. (eds) (2018). *David Hume on Morals, Politics, and Society*. New Haven and London: Yale University Press.

DiAngelo, R. (2019). *White Fragility*. United Kingdom: Penguin Books Ltd.

Foucault, M., & Sheridan, A. (1977). *Discipline and Punish: The Birth of the Prison*. London: Allen Lane.

Geronimus, A. T. (1992). The Weathering Hypothesis and the Health of African-American Women and Infants: Evidence and Speculations. *Ethnicity & Disease* 2(3), 207–221.

Geronimus, A. T. (1996). Black/White Differences in the Relationship of Maternal Age to Birthweight: A Population-Based Test of the Weathering Hypothesis. *Social Science & Medicine* 42(4), 589–597.

Geronimus, A. T., Hicken, M., Keene, D., & Bound, J. (2006). "Weathering" and Age Patterns of Allostatic Load Scores Among Blacks and Whites in the United States. *American Journal of Public Health* 96(5), 826–833. https://doi.org/10.2105/AJPH.2004.060749

Goleman, D. (2004). *Emotional Intelligence: Why It Can Matter More Than IQ & Working with Emotional Intelligence*. London: Bloomsbury.

Gray, H. (1995). Black Masculinity and Visual Culture. *Callaloo* 18(2), 401–405.

Kleingeld, P. (2007). Kant's Second Thoughts on Race. *The Philosophical Quarterly* 57, 573–592.

Long, E. (2002). *The History of Jamaica: Reflections on Its Situation, Settlements, Inhabitants, Climate, Products, Commerce, Laws and Government*. Montreal: McGill-Queen's University Press.

Murray, C., & Herrnstein, R. J. (1996). *The Bell Curve: Intelligence and Class Structure in American Life*. New York: Simon and Schuster University of North Carolina Press.

Painter, N. I. (2010). *The History of White People*. New York: W.W. Norton.

Phillips, K. W., Rothbard, N. P., & Dumas, T. L. (2009). To Disclose or Not to Disclose? Status Distance and Self-Disclosure in Diverse Environments. *Academy of Management Review* 34(4), 710–732.

Seaton, E. K., & Iida, M. (2019). Racial Discrimination and Racial Identity: Daily Moderation among Black Youth. *American Psychologist* 74, 117–127. https://doi.org/10.1037/amp0000367

Sibrava, N. J., Bjornsson, A. S., Perez Benitez, A. C. I., Moitra, E., Weisberg, R. B., & Keller, M. B. (2019). Posttraumatic Stress Disorder in African American and Latinx Adults: Clinical Course and the Role of Racial and Ethnic Discrimination. *American Psychologist* 74, 101–116. https://doi.org/10.1037/amp0000339

Slatton, B. C., & Spates, K. (eds) (2016). *Hyper Sexual, Hyper Masculine?: Gender, Race and Sexuality in the Identities of Contemporary Black Men*. London and New York: Routledge.

Sobczak, A. (2018). The Queen Bee Syndrome. The Paradox of Women Discrimination on the Labour Market. *Journal of Gender and Power* 51(1).

Staines, G., Tavris, C., & Jayaratne, T. E. (1974). The Queen Bee Syndrome. *Psychology Today* 7, 55–60.

Thomas, D. A., & Gabarro, J. J. (1999). *Breaking Through: The Making of Minority Executives in Corporate America*. Boston, MA: Harvard Business Review Press.

Williams, D. R., et al. (2019). Racism and Health: Evidence and Needed Research. *Annual Review of Public Health* 40(1), 105–125.

Wingfield, A. H. (2007). The Modern Mammy and the Angry Black Man: African American Professionals' Experiences with Gendered Racism in the Workplace. *Race, Gender & Class* 196–212.

5

"YOU ARE NOT ONE OF THE LOUD ONES"

This chapter

- *contextualises the Model Black as a new trope,*
- *describes the first of the three Model Black behaviours: squaring,*
- *outlines the impression tension that black leaders experience at work and*
- *examines the different ways in which squaring plays out in the work-place.*

The other thing I attribute my success to when I've actually been working is just sheer resilience because you have to be able to suppress a lot of stuff to get on and actually stay employed in the corporate workplace, I think, especially in the City, in London – you can't be Black.

Naomi, Senior Recruitment Consultant

I've managed to almost manoeuvre and [learn] how to work in a white environment and understand the white culture, but to that point, I lost a lot of my black culture. I think that is one huge regret I have in terms of being able to work so well in a certain culture, but I, kind of, lost friends, you know, people I've known because I didn't ever spend time with them because I was always trying to balance and work in this other kind of world.

Derek Bruce, Head of Leadership
Development, Signify

I don't bring my whole self to work just like lots of people of colour don't bring their whole selves to work because it's not

DOI: 10.4324/9781003200482-9

welcome and because it's not understood. There is no sense from white colleagues that we might live our lives differently outside the organisation. . . . I think that's really sad and that's something that needs to change because you can't bring your whole self to work. You don't feel valued for who you are.

Patricia Miller, OBE, Chief Executive NHS

Boris Johnson can come into work and be him and get away with it because there's all this privilege attached. A young Boris Johnson could come in and be as abrasive as he likes. If I came in and did the same, it would be all over the papers; my career would be finished.

David Lammy, MP

This is the first of three chapters describing the Model Black's behavioural strategies to navigate their work environment. These strategies of squaring, self-silencing and softening emerged from the research with 30 senior black British leaders. The following three chapters will discuss how each of these strategies plays out and examine the implications for the Model Black and their colleagues. It is important to note that these strategies form part of a normal way of being. It is also worth reiterating that the leaders do not regard themselves as victims but as successful individuals who have identified ways to "be" in order to thrive at work.

As discussed in Chapter 4 one of the most powerful reasons black leaders report needing to be the Model Black is that they are constantly fighting against the stereotypes within society about what it means to be racialised as black. These stereotypes relate to the racial tropes that have permeated our broader society.

THE MODEL BLACK: THE NEW TROPE

The Model Black provides a new trope for black British leaders. In Chapter 4, I introduced the nine elements that comprise the profile of the Model Black. The three behaviours of the Model Black (squaring, self-silencing and softening) are probably, at some level, a response to the negative racial tropes that have developed over hundreds of years. As shown in Figure 5.1, these behaviours combine to create the success strategies of the Model Black leader as viewed

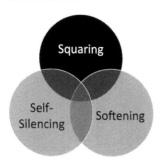

Figure 5.1 Squaring – a success strategy of the Model Black

from the perspective of non-black colleagues within the workplace. I take for granted that these behaviours take place in a context where the black leader is already overperforming in their role. Chapters 5, 6 and 7 discuss how each of these behavioural strategies plays out and examine the implications for the Model Black and their colleagues. Enacting these strategies to become the Model Black can contribute to the process of weathering (Chapter 4).

HOW BLACK LEADERS BE THE MODEL BLACK

Squaring

Squaring is the first behaviour the Model Black employs to navigate the white workplace. This is the process whereby the Model Black assimilates into a white middle-class way of being and plays down aspects of blackness. The leaders simultaneously understand how to behave in ways that their white colleagues recognise in themselves whilst ensuring that they do not conform to negative elements of the black British stereotype.

The cultural practices and ways of behaving are, at senior levels in organisations, typically designed by and advantage white middle-class males. By cultural practices, I mean the behavioural norms such as the way people talk to each other as well as the topics that people talk about, the ways individuals dress and the outside work activities that they are expected to take part in. This forms part of the culture that organisations possess and that all employees play a role in creating and sustaining. For the black leader, there can be the complication of coming from a different background with different norms and experiences. Many of these norms and experiences are, at best, not valued in the same way as the white middle-class experience and, at worst, seen as inferior. Whilst other groups like women, those from working-class backgrounds and members of the LGBTQ+ community also have to adapt to these norms, black leaders have to additionally work at the intersections of race with gender, class and sexuality.

The black leaders I spoke to recognised early in their careers that they need to be more like the white middle-class majority of leaders in order to succeed. The relative starting point for black leaders interviewed in their quest for similarity was different depending on their skin tone, their own upbringing and life experiences. Three of the interviewees who described themselves as "mixed-race" talked spontaneously about their recognition that they had a skin tone advantage. They were the acceptable face of blackness and diversity. One spoke about noticing that a darker-skinned, more competent colleague was not invited into client meetings and how it took that colleague years longer to be promoted in the professional services company where they both worked. These leaders of mixed heritage also talked about the benefit of being racially ambiguous. One, who currently works outside the UK, was often seen as southern European. In first meetings, his racial background proved to be a source of intrigue and interest. These leaders recognised their skin tone advantages whilst still identifying as black, yet recognised the daily challenges of not being viewed as white.

The black leaders who, on account of where they grew up or where they were educated, shared some of the cultural capital with white colleagues also started out ahead. They were often Deservers and Drivers. These leaders often sent their children to the same schools or lived in the same areas as their colleagues. They had a lot of similar reference points, watching the same films, visiting the same theatres. This made it much less of an effort for the white people around them. For these leaders, the process of squaring often required less effort.

In contrast, there were also black leaders who started on the back foot in terms of what they had in common with their white colleagues. These individuals had to work hardest at squaring in the workplace. In many cases, they made huge efforts to fit in and hide their black selves. Some did this consciously through observing and imitating white ways of being and behaving. Others worked hard to fit in, and only later in life did they reflect that this was something they had done without consciously thinking about it. When they did reflect, there was a sense that this had taken a toll on them. At some level, they had recognised the need to adapt because they understood that being black was associated with so many negative connotations. However, whether advantaged by skin colour, background or experience, the black leaders often recognised the need to fit in and play down their blackness.

How do I come across?

One aspect of squaring is constantly checking the impression that you are making on those around you. Typically, this involves looking for cues in the moment regarding how assertive or forceful you are being perceived. One in four of the leaders talked about times when they had been given feedback that behaviour that is tolerated and even encouraged in their white counterparts is unwelcome from them. One leader told me about a common experience that he had during meetings. He would be part of a group that was brainstorming ideas and challenging each other. It was an energetic meeting with lots of discussion with different individuals taking the lead. After the meeting, his manager would come up and say, "You made some really good points, but you don't have to be so aggressive in the meeting; you don't have to be so strong in the meeting. Let other people have their opinions. Don't try and scare them."

The black leader would be doing nothing different to his white peers, talking and contributing in exactly the same way. He would understand from this feedback that his manager did not want him jumping in, so he scaled back his participation in the meetings so that it did not look like he was any kind of aggressor. So, he sat back more and was then given the feedback that his contributions were not making it into the meeting. "I'm sitting in between two hard spaces, what do I do so I can't be perceived as aggressive, or else that's not going to get me promoted. When I pull back, I'm seen as not contributing. Navigating that one was hard. There was a lot of discussions about this conundrum in the black network meetings." He navigated this by asking his manager how best to participate.

"I would just ask and ask, 'Can you please let me know how you would have handled this situation? What techniques would you use?'" His manager went over the top offering him hours of advice! The black leader thanked his manager for "all of the great advice" and assured him he would act on it. This black leader claimed that such situations could be a big roadblock because if your manager dislikes you and feels you are aggressive, that is the one person who can ruin your entire career. He was well aware that if one person happens to be your boss, who does not take a liking to you, which could be just because of your ethnicity, you could be out. He had seen several black leaders who had failed to understand this corporate reality.

Similarly, a female leader talked about having to constantly weigh up how she was coming across. This was in a context where she was frequently hearing her team make subtle derogatory comments about her race. As a black female manager of people, she would have to think twice about how she was "landing." When she says "landing," she means ensuring that she was not coming across as too black. Too black meant anything that could be perceived as even marginally assertive. This situation made it challenging for her to manage her team. "How do I communicate effectively with this person without causing offence? Because I know they're playing up, they are undermining my authority, and I don't want it to come across as if I'm not sensitive to their needs." She would rethink almost every situation before she confronted it. She would rehearse every interaction. This worked for her, but it created a lot of hard work, which was very exhausting. It also meant that she could not ever be herself at work.

For black leaders, managing the impression tension (Figure 5.2) was a constant process of working on impact and impression so as to appear less like the stereotypes of blackness that their white colleagues and bosses possess. This became work. The Model Black navigates this space by using energy that could be better employed in doing the job well. Model Black leaders face the challenge of having to be more like white people through assimilation and be less like black people by "covering" (discussed in the following section).

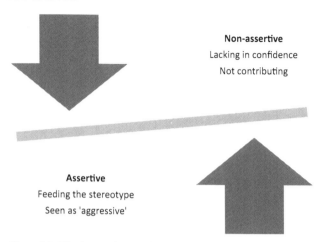

Non-assertive
Lacking in confidence
Not contributing

Assertive
Feeding the stereotype
Seen as 'aggressive'

Figure 5.2 The impression tension

Squaring through assimilation

A second aspect of squaring is assimilation. We all change our behaviour depending on our context. I behaved differently at the party of my five-year-old than I did when on an evening out with close girlfriends. That behaviour is also different from how I carry myself in the work environment. We all change our behaviour at work to abide by the social norms and thus fit in. One of the results of a failure to comply with the workplace norms is exclusion. Given the human desire to feel included, it makes sense to comply. Assimilation at work is, therefore, about behaving in ways so as to fit in with the ways of the dominant culture. For the Model Black leader, assimilation is the process of looking and acting "whiter and more middle-class." It is about embracing and adopting the attitudes, interests and behaviours of their white colleagues. As discussed previously, for some, this requires little adaptation. For others, it means a major shift and a lot of emotional labour.

The Model Black leader has to work at assimilation in order to fight against the negative racist stereotype of what a black British person is perceived to be in the broader society, as discussed in the earlier section on tropes. For black men, it is the stereotype of the hoodie-wearing criminal from the poor inner city who is poorly educated and speaks Jamaican patois. He wears gold jewellery, listens to rap music and is lazy, aggressive, coarse and hypersexed.[1] For the black woman, it is about being strong, angry and sexual.[2] She is loud, brash and difficult to get along with. For both black men and women, there are the added stereotypes that associate them with low levels of intelligence.

A third aspect of squaring is covering. Black leaders also "cover" or hide parts of themselves that they think may be less acceptable to the dominant culture. Covering was introduced by sociologist Erving Goffmann in 1963 in *Stigma*.[3] He describes how a person with a "stigma" may try to cover it to make it easier for themselves and others. Goffman cites the example of a girl who gets around best on her wooden limb but may use crutches or an artificial limb when in the presence of others. There are many public instances of covering, for example, Margaret Thatcher lowering the pitch of her voice. The concept of consciously changing the impression one is making to be more acceptable is not new. However, in the workplace, covering is problematic because it can have a negative effect on how individuals see themselves and because the energy used to cover is energy taken away from being productive.

Black people are far more likely to cover than their white counterparts. Research by Deloitte[4] showed that 79 per cent of black people cover compared to 45 per cent of straight white males. This reinforces the notion that those who set the cultural norms and run the organisation find it easiest to be themselves at work. According to Deloitte's study, covering can take four forms: Changing one's *appearance*, that is, grooming, attire or mannerisms to fit into the mainstream; distancing one's *affiliation* by avoiding behaviours that are associated with their identity; avoiding any *association* with other members of their group; and refraining from *advocating* for a group they belong to. The black leaders I spoke with gave examples of how squaring through assimilation and covering became key tools they employed to successfully navigate their workplaces. However, for some, using these tools became another weight they had to carry. Carrying this burden was seen as necessary for getting on at work.

Finding out what was of interest to your colleagues, actively learning more about it, and staying up to date on the subject was one way of assimilating. Paul Cleal, a former PwC partner we met in Chapter 2, talked about finding common ground. He spent weekends reading up so that he could know what happened in the rugby. That way, he would have something to say about it on Monday morning. Even though rugby "bores the pants off" him, he would at least know that England had beaten Scotland, and that was enough to show interest in other people. He recognised that is what people like:

> If you show interest in them, they think that you're nice. If you're genuinely interested, then that probably means you *are* nice. It's not hard to read the paper on the way into the office, work out that England beat Scotland on Saturday afternoon and something controversial happened that you can discuss with them later – and it helps to build a relationship. I've always done a bit of that, I guess. I think about what it is that other people are interested in, and how do you find your way into their group?

A female leader also talked about feigning interest in rugby. She would watch the Rugby World Cup, knowing that she would be able to have that conversation in the cafeteria. Not knowing meant that you would be excluded.

Accepting and embracing the pub and drinking culture was also an important way of assimilating. One teetotal black leader talked about making a real effort to go to the pub just to be friendly rather than out of any desire to sit in a room with the colleagues she had already spent an entire day with. "Standing in a bar with a beer in your hand is not part of Nigerian culture, but if I'm not there, they will notice." A senior leader in the advertising industry explained that his industry was so relational that if you do not like drinking in a pub, it creates a barrier between you and your colleagues and, ultimately, your clients.

Another leader, who found herself in the company of many women who had attended Benenden School, told me how she had bought several books on etiquette and studied them for hours. She needed to know what was expected from her in the company of these kinds of white women!

These issues around assimilating to fit in are not exclusive to black leaders. What is different for black leaders is firstly the feeling that all of the energy is one way – that is that white people are not making an effort to be curious about *their* interests. Secondly, that little thought is given to the fact that they might lead different lives or have other interests. There is not even the perception that there is a whole other cultural experience that merits exploration and discussion. The lack of curiosity can be crippling for the black leader and, in some cases, undermine their sense of self. The workplace thus serves as a place that reinforces the adage that you have to engage in particular forms of white cultural activities if you want to be successful. However, the Model Black understands and even embraces this. As advertising executive Jonathan Akwue explained:

> Any kind of perceived barrier can be a real obstacle for someone who doesn't come from the norm or who sits outside the norm. That was the thing that I had to learn to navigate because I came from an environment where I was completely comfortable, where I knew everything about it. I was absolutely in my comfort zone, and I had to move into a social environment that, quite frankly, I was not familiar with. I had to understand the nuances and the very subtle ways in which exclusion happens, which is so rarely spoken but often felt.

Squaring by covering[5]

The Model Black understands the importance of appearance. Black leaders talked about dressing smarter than their colleagues in order to succeed. This was partly because dressing well was part of their home culture but also because they did not want to conform to any negative stereotypes around black people's inability to look professional at work. There was a palpable sense that they would not be forgiven for not looking the part. A senior police officer told me that it was known that when she was out of uniform, she would wear nicely tailored double-breasted suits, pencil skirts, heels and stockings. "Could anyone ever say I was anything but smart in my clothes? They could not. I just was not a stereotype. I dressed differently. I looked different. I sounded different."

Then there is the issue of black women's hair. For the uninitiated, black women typically wear their hair in four ways. There is the realm of weaves and wigs which can be straight, curly or anything in between which is attached to their hair. Then there is the processed hair, which is hair that has been heated or treated with chemicals to take out some or all of the curls. There are the plaited extensions whereby artificial hair is plaited onto your own. Then there are the natural styles where hair is left in tight or looser natural curls. Chris Rock's documentary *Good Hair*[6] is a must-watch for any reader who would like a deeper understanding.

I was interviewing one senior leader on the weekend who had her shoulder-length hair in its natural state. She was keen to remind me that this was her weekend look and that when she went to the office on weekdays, she ensured that she had it straightened or tied back in order to be taken seriously. I was reminded of a conversation with a senior NHS leader who wore her hair in braided extensions. Her manager told her that she looked "very aggressive" when she wore her hair in this way. She never changed her hair but was always acutely aware of its impact on her boss. Then there is the tale of the woman whose mother insisted that she had her hair straightened for her interview for a professional services firm. She did not want to risk rejection on the basis of not being the "right fit." The Model Black woman is acutely aware that her white colleagues do not "get" black hair, so it becomes much easier to have it in a style that white people can connect with. She is aware that race becomes an issue when she changes her hair – especially if that change involves a shift from recognisable straight hair to a plaited or natural curly style. It was interesting that as the Model Black women I interviewed became more confident in their senior roles, they felt more able to move away from the Eurocentric expectations around hair and beauty.

However, it is important to state here that the issue of black hair, in particular, black women's hair, is complex and political.[7] Black women spend around three times the amount that white women do on their hair. Many black women have their hair straight because that is how they choose to wear it. There is a school of thought that any black hairstyle that takes the hair away from its natural, thick kinks represents a black woman's "selling-out" – an attempt to become more white. However, this is not the case for black leaders because they are making a positive decision on how they choose to wear their hair.

When it comes to how they talk, the Model Black leader knows that he has to speak like his middle-class white peers. One leader told me how he did everything in his power to lose his accent, having been an ardent jafaican (a dialect spoken in London, influenced by Jamaica patois). However, he also had to deal with the tension of his black identity being both a problem because of its negative associations with crime and laziness and yet also regarded as cool.

Model black leaders do not complain about making these changes. This is about navigating and succeeding. Black leaders are not actively thinking about the stereotypes they are working to avoid. They are conditioned to understand what it takes to get to the top and stay there. Appearance is critical; it is about first impressions, about whether you are visually fit to be amongst your white peers. The difficulty is that decisions about what appearance is acceptable is ultimately not in the hands of the black leaders but their white colleagues.

Squaring by avoiding affiliation

Chris Forbes is a senior executive in global consultancy. Relaxed, sensitive and cheerful, it seems he drops a punchline every few sentences. He told me how he worked as a DJ at weekends. He made a conscious decision to keep this very quiet at work. The idea that his colleagues would know that he was spinning discs in black clubs at the weekend whilst they were on the golf course or playing tennis was unimaginable. The potential fallout could be career limiting. Chris was trying to ensure that his professionalism was taken seriously and did not want to be cornered in the corridor by junior colleagues, telling him how much they enjoyed his gig. He tells me the amusing story of a time when he joined an American Bank. "I remember I was literally in the lavatory, standing up against the urinal, and a very junior black guy stood next to me. He said, 'Have you got a twin brother who is a DJ.'" Chris was horrified and felt as though he had been exposed. He wishes that he had been able to be proud of his hobby and able to share his weekend passion with his colleagues. However, he was aware of the potential of the negative stereotype. There was no reason to take the risk. His experience is in sharp contrast to a white 40-something I know of who also DJs at weekends. The reactions to his hobby are geared more towards curiosity about what kinds of '80s music he plays and what time the dancing stops!

Avoiding affiliation with the stereotype also means being far better at your job than your white counterparts in order to be treated equally by them. This idea of being better to be equal is a common refrain in all black households, the oft-repeated mantra of the black parent. This manifests itself for the Model Black leader in having to be overqualified for the job. I sometimes think it is no accident that I possess five degrees! The model black leader further talks about actively taking care not to make a mistake. They will take additional time to check over their work, knowing that any mistake will be amplified. This brings additional pressures: "You're not allowed to make any mistakes whatsoever: Working is very stressful for me because you've just got to be on point with absolutely everything . . . having to do everything really, really diligently."

What is noticeable is this layering of pressures on the black leader. The Model Black takes this in her stride. She accepts the layers, recognising that this is the unavoidable path to success. She also knows how much more she could offer her employer if she did not have to take on this additional burden.

Squaring by avoiding association

The Model Black leader sometimes thinks carefully about associating with other blacks. First, there is the concern that you are seen as "too black." Secondly, they want to avoid any association with any negative perceptions white colleagues may have of that individual. There is the awkward moment that I used to experience on the extremely rare occasions that I saw another black leader in the room at a business meeting. The first thought was, I hope that they are good and will not let the side down. I know that if a black person does not perform well enough, there will be a perception that all black people are bad. Then follows the question, should I go up to them and have a conversation? If I go up to them immediately, then the white people in the room might think that I am too black, and if I approach the black leader, and it transpires that the black person is not an outstanding performer, then I am immediately associated with their poor performance. So, the beeline approach is out. Maybe the casual approach during the coffee break. Not sure. There is still the risk that she might be thinking the same as me: concerned that I am a poor performer and thinks it best to avoid being too close to me. Maybe the best way to navigate this is to ignore her for the time being! Knowing that blackness still has negative associations even at senior levels, the Model Black leader takes care to keep the correct distance. Like the SCAN process of weighing up potentially offensive remarks I discussed in Chapter 1, this decision can take a lot of emotional energy.

Some years ago, I was asked to find an executive coach for a senior black leader working at board level in healthcare. I looked through my network and found two candidates I thought would be great chemistry for her. They were both independent coaches, one of them was black, and the other was white. Both sent through their resumes, and the black leader had an initial chemistry conversation with them. She made her choice and selected the white coach. I caught up with her to find out which one she had chosen and why. She explained that intuitively she felt that the black coach would be better for her. However, she knew that if she had a black coach, her boss would feel that she was not taking the issue of coaching seriously enough. Her boss could not perceive that a black coach could be sufficiently professional to support her through complex strategic and leadership issues. Why would she work with her coach of choice and risk her career?

Another black leader in a large global services company felt it was best to avoid joining black worker organisations. He could see the value in them. They provided a great space for black employees to share challenges and consider how to improve equity and inclusion. However, on a personal level, he was reluctant because he saw them as spaces where black workers went to complain and share negative stories. He never saw himself as a victim. Therefore, he made the conscious decision that navigating successfully as a black man meant not associating himself with the "victim" blacks.

Model black leaders also learn that being in groups with other blacks makes white people feel uncomfortable. One leader described a time when he thought it would be nice to meet up with some black folks for lunch. It was lunch with five other black people who worked on the same site. He told me (with some humour) that as they sat at the table, non-black employees kept coming over to ask what was going on. "What do you mean what's going on?" he thought. "Because I didn't even register, and then later, I remembered somebody coming over once before and saying, 'Oh! This is black lunch!' And another saying, 'Is this a coup being planned or something?'" Recognising the discomfort that this caused his colleagues, he thought very carefully about organising such a meeting on the site again.

So, the Model Black becomes an expert at squaring through assimilation and covering. This is necessary because the stereotypes that exist in society are brought into the workplace. We know that representations of race and ethnicity are not neutral categories. As discussed in Chapter 4, they are imbued with ideas that have been developed over hundreds of years which come with notions of superiority and inferiority. The Model Black recognises this and chooses to be willing, cognisant participants. However, participation does not mean that there is not huge frustration at having to use energy to get approval from white people.

The cost is significant for black leaders and their workplaces. On the one hand, the Model Black represents a kind of black excellence that should be celebrated. They are in a position to challenge the negative racist stereotypes about black people. On the other hand, this imposes a huge weight that contributes to weathering (Chapter 4). Black leaders also know that this is a weight that their white counterparts do not have to carry and consequently can succeed with much less effort.

KEY TAKEAWAYS

- The Model Black is hyperconscious of how they come across – ensuring that they behave in a way that makes white people feel comfortable.
- The Model Black successfully navigates the workplace by finding ways of being more like their white middle-class colleagues.
- This process of squaring can demand a lot of energy from black leaders.

QUESTIONS FOR REFLECTION

- How much genuine curiosity do you show about your black colleagues' lives outside of work?
- To what extent are you truly open to ways of behaving differently from your organisation's "norm?"
- What can you do to ensure that you are not demanding more from your black colleagues than from others?

NOTES

1 Chapple, R. L., Jacinto, G. A., Harris-Jackson, T. N., & Vance, M. (2017). Do# BlackLivesMatter? Implicit Bias, Institutional Racism and Fear of the Black Body. *Ralph Bunche Journal of Public Affairs* 6(1), 2; Doss, A. (2013). Black Bodies, White Spaces: Understanding the Construction of White Identity through the Objectification and Lynching of Black Bodies. *Black Diaspora Review* 3(2), 14–17; Gray, H. (1995). Black Masculinity and Visual Culture. *Callaloo* 18(2), 401–405.

2 Collins, P. H. (1991). Controlling Images and Black Women's Oppression. *Seeing Ourselves: Classic, Contemporary, and Cross-Cultural Readings in Sociology* 4, 266–273; Collins, P. H. (2000). *Black Feminist Thought: Knowledge, Consciousness, and the Politics of Empowerment*. London and New York: Routledge.

3 Goffman, E. (1963). *Stigma: Notes on the Management of Spoiled Identity*. Englewood Cliffs, NJ: Prentice-Hall Edition.

4 Deloitte. (2019). *Uncovering Talent: A New Model of Inclusion*. https://www2.deloitte.com/us/en/pages/about-deloitte/articles/covering-in-the-work place.html [Last accessed 23 July 2021].

5 Yoshino, K. (2007). *Covering: The Hidden Assault on Our Civil Rights*. New York: Random House Trade Paperbacks.

6 Stilson, J. (2009). *Good Hair*. Chris Rock Productions, HBO Films.

7 Dabiri, E. (2019). *Don't Touch My Hair*. London: Allen Lane; Dawson, G., & Karl, K. (2018). I Am Not My Hair, or Am I? Examining Hair Choices of Black Female Executives. *Journal of Business Diversity* 18(2).

REFERENCES AND ADDITIONAL READING

Chapple, R. L., Jacinto, G. A., Harris-Jackson, T. N., & Vance, M. (2017). Do# BlackLivesMatter? Implicit Bias, Institutional Racism and Fear of the Black Body. *Ralph Bunche Journal of Public Affairs* 6(1), 2.

Collins, P. H. (1991). Controlling Images and Black Women's Oppression. *Seeing Ourselves: Classic, Contemporary, and Cross-Cultural Readings in Sociology* 4, 266–273.

Collins, P. H. (2000). *Black Feminist Thought: Knowledge, Consciousness, and the Politics of Empowerment.* London and New York: Routledge.

Dabiri, E. (2019). *Don't Touch My Hair.* London: Allen Lane.

Dawson, G., & Karl, K. (2018). I Am Not My Hair, or Am I? Examining Hair Choices of Black Female Executives. *Journal of Business Diversity* 18(2).

Deloitte. (2019). *Uncovering Talent: A New Model of Inclusion.* https://www2.deloitte.com/us/en/pages/about-deloitte/articles/covering-in-the-workplace.html [Last accessed 23 July 2021].

Doss, A. (2013). Black Bodies, White Spaces: Understanding the Construction of White Identity through the Objectification and Lynching of Black Bodies. *Black Diaspora Review* 3(2), 14–17.

Fanon, F. (2008). *Black Skin, White Masks.* United Kingdom: Grove Press.

Gaither, S. E., Babbitt, L. G., & Sommers, S. R. (2018). Resolving Racial Ambiguity in Social Interactions. *Journal of Experimental Social Psychology* 76, 259–269.

Gilbert, D. (2005). Interrogating Mixed-Race: A Crisis of Ambiguity? *Social Identities* 11(1), 55–74.

Goff, P. A., Steele, C. M., & Davies, P. G. (2008). The Space between Us: Stereotype Threat and Distance in Interracial Contexts. *Journal of Personality and Social Psychology* 94, 91–107.

Goffman, E. (1963). *Stigma: Notes on the Management of Spoiled Identity.* Englewood Cliffs, NJ: Prentice-Hall Edition.

Gray, H. (1995). Black Masculinity and Visual Culture. *Callaloo* 18(2), 401–405.

Hall, J. C., Everett, J., & Hamilton-Mason, J. (2011, June). Black Women Talk About Workplace Stress and How They Cope. *Journal of Black Studies* 43(2). Knoxville, TN: University of Tennessee.

Johnson, T. A., & Bankhead, T. (2014). Hair It Is: Examining the Experiences of Black Women with Natural Hair. *Open Journal of Social Sciences* 2, 86–100.

Joseph-Salisbury, R., & Connelly, L. (2018). 'If Your Hair Is Relaxed, White People Are Relaxed. If Your Hair Is Nappy, They're Not Happy': Black Hair as a Site of 'Post-Racial' Social Control in English Schools. *Social Sciences* 7(11), 219.

Kleingeld, P. (2007). Kant's Second Thoughts on Race. *The Philosophical Quarterly* 57, 573–592.

Lewis, J. A., Mendenhall, R., Harwood, S. A., & Browne Huntt, M. (2016). "Ain't I a Woman?" Perceived Gendered Racial Microaggressions Experienced by Black Women. *The Counseling Psychologist* 44(5), 758–780.

Lewis, J. A., Mendenhall, R., Harwood, S. A., & Huntt, M. B. (2013). Coping with Gendered Racial Microaggressions among Black Women College Students. *Journal of African American Studies* 17(1), 51–73.

Patton, T. O. (2006). Hey Girl, Am I More Than My Hair?: African American Women and Their Struggles with Beauty, Body Image, and Hair. *NWSA Journal* 24–51.

Rosette, A. S., & Dumas, T. L. (2007). The Hair Dilemma: Conform to Mainstream Expectations or Emphasize Racial Identity. *Duke Journal of Gender Law & Policy* 14, 407.

Sims, J. P., & Njaka, C. L. (2019). *Mixed-Race in the US and UK: Comparing the Past, Present, and Future.* United Kingdom: Emerald Group Publishing.

Yoshino, K. (2007). *Covering: The Hidden Assault on Our Civil Rights.* New York: Random House Trade Paperbacks.

6

"YOU ARE NOT CHIPPY"

This chapter

- *describes the second of the three Model Black behaviours: self-silencing,*
- *explains the Model Black's four choices when responding to racism and*
- *considers the energy equation of staying silent versus speaking out.*

You're invisible, you're not seen. When you speak, people ignore you. You don't have any credibility. If you get anything wrong, it's picked over like it's a big deal. You can't show any sort of emotion or anything. You're belittled. Your race is belittled, your class is belittled, and you're expected to just take it, and if you don't, people think that you've got an attitude.

Anon, Senior Executive, Financial Services

There were a couple of occasions where I experienced racism in politics. Not a couple, a few. Institutional, from people much more senior to me. The one occasion, where I called it what it was to another colleague, a white colleague, rather. I realized, when the conversation was shut down, I was never going to do that again. I'm never going to put myself in such a vulnerable position because it was clear to me that even close colleagues, people I considered friends, did not understand what the hell I was talking about.

David Lammy, MP

It better be really extreme for you to be able to go down that path because once you open that door, there's no closing it, and

DOI: 10.4324/9781003200482-10

your name could be mud in a world in which you need references to get that next job. You want to get to the next career, you need references. If you've gone to your employer and accused a few senior partners of racism, sexism, or whatever, and those people don't get fired, they're still at the firm, or their friends are still at the firm, you're screwed when that reference call comes in.

Anon, Senior Executive, Technology

There are sometimes things that are just outright wrong that you will have to challenge, but you can often mostly do those things in a way that is still professional doesn't allow you to become a caricature or cliche.

Robyn Williams, Metropolitan
Police Superintendent

Ignore? I don't think you can ever ignore because you – what I've learned is that if you ignore things, you stockpile them. They begin to weigh heavily on you. The response has to be commensurate with what has happened and how best to deal with that.

Anon, Senior Manager, Public Sector

SELF-SILENCING AT WORK

The second strategy adopted by the Model Black is self-silencing their response to unacceptable racially offensive behaviour, from so-called microaggressions[1] to overt racism. The Model Black recognises (often early in their career) that there is a stark choice to be made between responding to racially motivated behaviour at work or ignoring it. So how does the Model Black respond? The black leaders I interviewed talked about this speaking-out dilemma in relation to offensive incidents: damned or labelled if you do, stressed if you do not. The Model Black also recognises that the consequences of speaking out are rarely positive. They learn that, in almost every case, it makes sense to let things go. Ignore it and move on. The process of coming to this decision does require some emotional effort. The Model Black works through the SCAN model, weighing up the Situation, Confirming what has happened, Analysing to

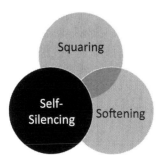

Figure 6.1 Self-silencing – a success strategy of the Model Black

decide on Next steps. The Model Black has criteria against which they make decisions at each stage. How do they decide what to do at the "next" stage? One of the decisions is whether to respond or self-silence. Responding invariably ends badly. Of the 30 leaders I spoke to, I heard only two examples of when responding to inappropriate behaviour did not result in negative relations with colleagues. The emotional labour required to preserve those relationships was phenomenal.

The Model Black does not respond to every comment or racist incident. They know that much of what offends them is unintentional. Through a combination of developing a thick skin and selective hearing, they are able to ignore most comments.

TO SPEAK OR NOT TO SPEAK?

What are the considerations that the Model Black has that influence whether they want to respond or self-silence? First, there is potential to be labelled an agitator or part of the "politically correct" police. Allied to this is the perception that they are playing the "race card," using their colour to benefit them and cause discomfort to their white colleagues. Second, there is concern about the negative impact on relationships with colleagues. You can lose friends and make enemies very quickly as colleagues close ranks when a perceived outsider raises an issue about one of them. This is especially the case when someone who looks different is perceived to attack one of their own. Third, there is a concern as to what all of this means for career progression. More than half of the black leaders interviewed expressed concern that confronting bad behaviour in any way would have a negative impact on their careers. The final consideration was one of personal pride. Could I live with myself if I allowed comments to remain unchallenged? What might be the effect on my sense of self and the long-term impact on my mental health?

The Model Black is right to be concerned. Studies from the US indicate that black leaders who want to progress within organisations know not to speak out about bias or racism at work because they may be labelled "agitators."[2] Indeed, research shows that minorities are often criticised for actively promoting diversity.[3] As I researched this book, I struggled to find leaders who still wanted to progress within their organisations that were prepared to publicly put their names to comments that were even mildly critical of their organisations. This is understandable. This self-censoring may be strategically smart behaviour on the part of the Model Black.

However, this self-silencing may have a negative impact on organisations. The effect of black leaders feeling that they cannot speak out is that they become disconnected. The 2017[4] study by the Center for Talent Innovation showed that those who are unable to speak out often feel more isolated in the workplace than those who speak freely, are nearly three times as likely to consider leaving the organisation and are 13 times as likely to be disengaged.

ASSUME POSITIVE INTENT

The Model Black leaders emphasised that they did not go around looking for racism under every rock. By and large, they assumed positive intent from their colleagues and did not presume ill will or malice in the workplace. They liked to operate from a position of good faith. Positive intent was assumed regardless of the nature of the incident. These incidents could be any action or words that communicated something negative towards black people. These included racial jokes, comments that suggested discriminatory messages ("you speak such good English") and comments that undermined their daily reality ("stop over-reacting").

However, one leader described the difficulty in always assuming positive intent as having the same mildly irritating joke told about you over and over again. The first time you might tolerate it and even laugh, but by the sixth or seventh time, you feel ready to punch the person in the face. This is what it is like repeatedly experiencing microaggressions. It may be the first time a particular white colleague had behaved in this manner, but it may be the tenth, 50th or 100th time a black person had had to deal with this. So, even though the Model Black was assuming positive intent, this did not negate their feelings of hurt, injustice, exasperation and even exhaustion when unpleasant incidents occurred. They simply recognised that any other way of being would consume even more emotional energy and could damage their careers.

When on the receiving end of offensive behaviour, what are the choices open to black leaders, and why does the Model Black usually choose to self-silence? The black leader faces four key choices: "suck it up," deal with it in the moment, make an informal complaint or pursue a formal complaint. The "suck it up" option is complete self-silencing. Each of the other three options also requires a degree of self-silencing. The Model Black typically completely self-silences because the outcome of responding another way is very often negative. Each strategy has consequences.

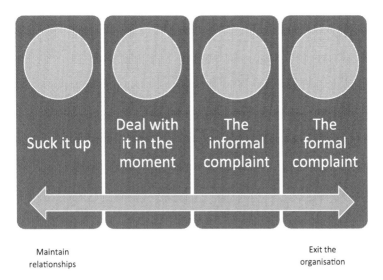

| Suck it up | Deal with it in the moment | The informal complaint | The formal complaint |

Maintain relationships

Exit the organisation

Figure 6.2 How the Model Black self-silences

Strategy 1: "Suck it up"

The first strategy is to "suck it up." This involves making a deliberate decision not to respond to the comment or behaviour in the moment or later. So, the incident is left completely unchallenged. However, there are consequences to allowing this to happen. Chris Forbes, the senior executive we met in Chapter 5, told me about the situation he found himself in. He was on an evening out with colleagues and potential clients in Bradford, a city where one in four of the population describe themselves as Asian. He was the only person of colour as the crowd stood drinking together. The more alcohol his colleagues and the clients drank, the more they started to talk about the things they found difficult with the local community. The comments were clearly aimed at the Asian community, although this was not overtly mentioned. The client talked about the difficulty in finding people who live nearby and who are the right fit for the organisation. This was particularly difficult when looking for young employees. As they consumed more alcohol, the conversation extended into negative comments about black people. Again, here the conversation was about people with different values, about experiences outside work where they have felt threatened when meeting people from other cultures. "Why can't they just dress like us?" There was lots of raucous laughter. Chris's SCAN led him to decide that there was no point in making any comment. They were in the company of a client, and it looked like they were about to secure a significant piece of business. Instead of making any comment at all, Chris found himself listening and nodding understandably, almost sympathetically with them. "It was not my proudest moment," he told me.

The impact of this on Chris was a feeling of deep shame. Shame in the workplace has been described as "a painful emotion that arises when an employee evaluates a threat to the self when he or she has fallen short of an important standard tied to a work-related identity."[5] This is the feeling that they have failed to live up to the way they define themselves in terms of their characteristics, relationships and classification in groups. Shame is about evaluating yourself negatively, seeing yourself as a bad person. Chris experienced shame because he felt he was letting down other people of colour. To stand by and allow such negative comments to be made completely unchallenged made him feel less of a person. It is sad that in a situation where Chris was not to blame for the comments, he was left with this feeling of inadequacy and self-loathing. For Chris, this feeling lasted overnight, then dissipated. He was able to put it to the back of his mind and convince himself that he had done the right thing in this situation. What might have been the consequences of speaking out in the moment? He would have embarrassed the company in front of a key client. What would have been the point in bringing it up the following day with his colleagues? He wanted to feel like he was part of the group, and this might jeopardise that relationship.

This event did have a long-term effect on the way in which Chris saw his colleagues. He realised that they possessed a lot of biases and prejudices against people of colour. He started to question how they might see him in the workplace. Did they see him as someone who did not really fit? Did they differentiate him from other black people who they saw as threatening and who they would never employ? Chris did not see his colleagues as bad people, but he was reminded of how engrained bias and prejudice can be and how differently they saw the world. As Chris told me the story, he mentioned that this was also a reminder that although he had made a lot of effort to be "one of the crowd" and be accepted by his colleagues, there would always be something that stood between him and them. This was not necessarily something he thought about every moment of every day. However, the experience did create a sense of distance between himself and them. He had a sense that there was a cloud that constantly hovered over his relationship with this particular group.

Strategy 2: Deal with it in the moment

There are cases where the Model Black feels that they can deal with comments in the moment. One female leader, Tracey, told me about an experience she had had with a colleague, Edward. They were travelling together and were outside the offices of one of their major clients. As the taxi arrived to pick them up, he glanced at one of the clients, then at Tracey, then commented to one of their hosts that he "only brought Tracey along to carry his bags." As she stood waiting for the taxi, Tracey was busy SCANning. She had decided she did not want to let this one go. She would raise this comment with her colleague. However, she noticed her temperature change, but she would not react in anger. So, she took a moment to calm herself as she knew that she had to stay focussed to bring up the issue. She also knew that she had to do it now before they went on to the next meeting, and this was all over. Her colleague was shocked that he had offended her and apologised. They never discussed it again. On the surface, things appeared normal between them, but Tracey found it hard to let go of the experience.

It was not just about the situation. How did her colleague really see her? She had felt that they were partners in the work that they were doing together, but these comments suggested that he regarded himself as somehow superior. Did this perception of her being inferior on account of her colour carry over to other aspects of the work that they did together? She would never find out. She felt she had dealt with the issue in the moment and was confident that such a comment would never be made again – at least not in her presence.

Here lies one of the dilemmas around speaking out. Is it enough to indicate that the comment was hurtful and not appropriate? Or do you take a lot more time to explain why this is the case? Often if white people have not done any work on themselves and their own identities and cannot recognise some of the challenges of being a minority in such a conversation, it can be difficult. Such conversations can demand a lot of emotional labour with no guarantee that they will improve matters in the long term. Consequently, the Model Black thinks very carefully about entering into any such conversation.

Strategy 3: The informal complaint

The Model Black thinks extremely carefully about raising any kind of informal complaint. As indicated in the quotes at the beginning of this chapter, this can be a one-directional path to career disaster. None of the leaders I spoke with cited a positive experience.

It was a Friday evening, and Naomi, the senior recruitment consultant who we met in Chapter 4, was finishing off her admin for the week. She could hear a guy who was a graduate trainee being really rude to one of the girls on her team. She playfully suggested he read a book that would help with his business communication. He turned to her and said in a calm, matter-of-fact way, "Why don't you go back to where you came from." She got up out of her seat because she was so shocked. However, she remained calm. She sat in the ladies toilet for the next 20 minutes. Later, two of her white colleagues said they had heard what was said and felt that she had handled the situation well in the moment. However, they felt it was serious and that she should complain. They would support her. Over the course of the weekend, Naomi spoke with her black friends and decided she would go ahead. This was not the first racially motivated attack by the young man she had been subject to, and if the worst happened, she was very employable in the City.

On Monday, Naomi told the director what had happened. There was no sense from the director that something negative had happened. No questioning as to how Naomi felt. On the contrary, Naomi felt like *she* had done something wrong in raising the issue. Naomi was asked what she wanted to be done about this comment. In that moment, she felt immensely pressured and suggested an apology from the colleague. When the apology arrived, it was couched in so many ifs – "if I said something. . .," "if I offended you . . ." – that it felt more like a defence than an apology. Naomi had to decide whether she would accept this lame apology. To do so would mean accepting that the colleague's outburst was acceptable. She explained to the perpetrator that she was still feeling upset and sent him a link to an article from the *Independent* about Brexit and racial abuse. She also explained that his use of language was against company policy. Result? He broke down in tears, and the director told Naomi that she was being very aggressive. She said,

> I looked at the director, and I thought, "Bingo. Here we go." Because that's what you think, isn't it? That's what you really think. You just think this is a lot of nonsense. Racist abuse isn't taken seriously. That is why I wouldn't complain about it. I became annoyed with myself for taking things seriously. Because they had a Head of Diversity, I fell into the trap of complaining when I really should have done nothing. All I did by complaining was expose myself and give myself more stress and more trauma. It would have been better to just leave it.

One of the reasons the Model Black realises there is no point in complaining is because these issues are seldom taken seriously by senior management or HR. Ultimately, you, the black person, become the problem. They know that the outcome is isolation and damage to their reputations. Self-silencing makes better sense.

The Model Black has either experienced such a situation or heard about it from someone else and, in many cases, senses that pursuing anything vaguely "on the record" will provoke white fragility on the part of the organisation. The consequence is that the organisation cannot respond objectively because it is incensed that an accusation of racism has been made against one of their white colleagues.

Strategy 4: The formal complaint

Once you get to this stage of a formal complaint, the advice from other blacks is to seriously start to think about what you would like your exit package to look like. You need to be looking outside the company if you take things this far. It is very difficult to find out how many senior black leaders this has happened to because their exit packages are drafted so that they are unable to speak publicly about what has happened. Such contracts are necessarily there to ensure silence post-departure. However, I spoke with three people who had signed compromise agreements. One had received payoffs from four institutions in the City. Another contributor was still going through a formal process, over a year after her first complaint.

The black leaders I spoke to feel that once they go to the formal complaint stage, they lose control of the situation. Leaders talked about being caught up in a huge HR wheel of bureaucracy that continually snowballed. A formal complaint became a "war of attrition" with the organisation ducking and diving to avoid any sniff of racist behaviour and the individual black leader having to make a decision about if and when to drop the issue.

Linda works for a global manufacturer. The office is a very casual space where there is often a lot of chatter and banter. It is invariably light humoured, which is one of the reasons she enjoys being in this organisation. Two new recruits have recently joined the team, and she notices that their comments are a little too "on the edge" of being racially offensive. She starts to wonder whether this is intentional but puts that to the back of her mind. One morning, she comes in and notices that the communal fruit bowl has been moved to be near her desk, and the new colleagues have brought bananas.

It's a little odd but nothing to be concerned about. Then the discussions start to sound a little different. They talk about the wine that they've been drinking at the weekend that's called Coon. Linda feels uneasy, but what can she say? Then one of them tells a joke about the fact that he thought only drug dealers drove the same make of car as she does. Linda does not laugh. Finally, there is the incident of the gig. They talk about a band they had seen at the weekend who used the "N" word in its performance. They repeat the "N" word several times. Linda asks them not to use that word, as she feels it is offensive. Linda feels angry and humiliated. They tell the story again the next day. Something has to be done to stop this pattern of behaviour, so she complains to her line manager. He suggests she is being a little too sensitive. It is just office banter. She should just ignore the comments. Recognising that this is a pattern, not a single event, she decides to take it "formal." She checks the staff handbook and makes a written complaint to her line manager.

Her line manager carries out the first investigation and, unsurprisingly, finds that there had not been any breach of company policy. Linda is not happy, so she takes her complaint to the next level, HR. They launch an investigation in which all of the parties are interviewed. Versions of what happened differ. However, the colleagues are asked to apologise to her. Linda awaits the apologies. Four weeks later, she is advised that, with the support of their line manager, they have appealed the sanction and no longer need to apologise. Linda is now feeling disappointed and upset and takes some time off work. She decides to go through the appeals process. She knows that this move will take a lot of mental effort and pit her against her manager and potentially the other senior managers. But she feels she has no choice. The issue is now moved to a senior manager outside the department. There are more interviews. We are now six months into the process, and Linda is ostracised at work. The appeal is unsuccessful, as versions now differ even more widely. Linda is mentally exhausted and again takes time off sick. Whilst she is off sick, a compromise agreement is made with HR.

Linda's experience illustrates why the Model Black knows not to "go formal." "All you want is an apology and for all this nonsense to stop. Instead, you are made to feel like a troublemaker. I feel like I've been raped in public and now being asked to prove it. Why couldn't they just apologise and say this kind of behaviour cannot be tolerated?"

When I was interviewing for the book, I was hopeful of being able to share a single story where there was a positive outcome from speaking out so I could present a balanced picture of how black leaders could raise an issue and still walk around the organisation with their heads held high. I was left with the thought that perhaps there is something about white fragility which means that it is difficult for an organisation to truly accept and then reflect on the racist behaviour of its employees. Then, towards the end of the interviews, I found one! Grace Ononiwu CBE, Director of Legal Services at Crown Prosecution Service, told me of an experience from her first managerial role when she was confronted with an envelope that contained a cartoon caricature of a prisoner bound over, gagged, and chained and shaded in brown. On the top of it, it had the name of the unit that she led. She confronted this head-on, calling in the whole unit to discuss it and the Dignity at Work Policy. She believed that you have to be courageous and do the right thing in such situations. She had a good outcome and has subsequently had many promotions. Her experience was rare but showed that controlled and well-managed confrontation occasionally works. She also had the privilege of being the manager of the whole unit. My conversations with leaders did not surface similar examples in any private-sector companies.

Black leaders are doing extra work in the workplace SCANing, experiencing Jolts and making difficult decisions about when and how to speak out. This can be difficult emotional work. It can contribute to the concept of weathering discussed in Chapter 4. Equally, black leaders recognise this is part of the package of being part of getting to the top of organisations. They continue to work hard and power through.

KEY TAKEAWAYS

- The Model Black leaders do not respond to most of the racially offensive comments or behaviour they experience at work.
- The Model Black leaders assume positive intent in their daily interactions with their white colleagues.
- The Model Black leaders often do not perceive that they can call out racist behaviour without causing damage to their reputations at work.

QUESTIONS FOR REFLECTION

- How do you respond when you see or hear unacceptable behaviour in your workplace?
- To what extent does your organisation's culture allow individuals to complain about racist behaviour without fear of retribution?
- How have you responded when you heard that an individual had complained about racism?
- Has anyone ever suggested that your behaviour was unacceptable on account of your use of racially unacceptable language? How did you respond?

NOTES

1 Sue, D. W., & Spanierman, L. (2020). *Microaggressions in Everyday Life.* Hoboken, NJ: John Wiley & Sons.
2 Hewlett, S. A. et al. (2017, July). People Suffer at Work When They Can't Discuss the Racial Bias They Face Outside of It. *Harvard Business Review.* https://hbr.org/2017/07/people-suffer-at-work-when-they-cant-discuss-the-racial-bias-they-face-outside-of-it [Last accessed 24 July 2021].
3 Johnson, S. K., & Hekman, D. R. (2017). Women and Minorities Are Penalized for Promoting Diversity. *Harvard Business Review.* https://hbr.org/2016/03/women-and-minorities-are-penalized-for-promoting-diversity [Last accessed 24 July 2021].
4 Johnson, S. K., & Hekman, D. R. (2017). Women and Minorities Are Penalized for Promoting Diversity. *Harvard Business Review.* https://hbr.org/2016/03/women-and-minorities-are-penalized-for-promoting-diversity [Last accessed 24 July 2021].
5 Daniels, M. A., & Robinson, S. L. (2019). The Shame of It All: A Review of Shame in Organizational Life. *Journal of Management* 45(6), 2448–2473. doi:10.1177/0149206318817604.

REFERENCES AND ADDITIONAL READING

Abrams, J. A., Hill, A., & Maxwell, M. (2019). Underneath the Mask of the Strong Black Woman Schema: Disentangling Influences of Strength and Self-Silencing on Depressive Symptoms among US Black Women. *Sex Roles* 80(9), 517–526.

Ahmed, S. (2009). Embodying Diversity: Problems and Paradoxes for Black Feminists. *Race Ethnicity and Education* 12(1), 41–52.

Antoine, G. E., Kushlev, K., Schaumberg, R., & Zhong, R. (2020). Shame at Work: Multiple Conceptualizations of Shame and Its Impact on Individual Outcomes. In *Academy of Management Proceedings* (Vol. 2020, No. 1, p. 18371). Briarcliff Manor, NY 10510: Academy of Management.

Bowen, F., & Blackmon, K. (2003). Spirals of Silence: The Dynamic Effects of Diversity on Organizational Voice. *Journal of Management Studies* 40(6), 1393–1417.

Daniels, M. A., & Robinson, S. L. (2019). The Shame of It All: A Review of Shame in Organizational Life. *Journal of Management* 45(6), 2448–2473. https://doi.org/10.1177/0149206318817604.

Fitzgerald, T. D. (2017). Speaking Truth to Power: Black Educators' Perspectives on Challenging Racial Injustice Through the Lens of Systemic Racism Theory. In *Systemic Racism* (pp. 111–140). New York: Palgrave Macmillan.

Fleming, M. A 2nd., Scott, E. J., Bradford, P. S., Lattimore, C. M., Omesiete, W. I., Williams, C. A., & Martin, A. N. (2021). The Risk and Reward of Speaking Out for Racial Equity in Surgical Training. *Journal of Surgical Education* 78(5), 1387–1392.

Fox, S., & Stallworth, L. E. (2005). Racial/Ethnic Bullying: Exploring Links between Bullying and Racism in the US Workplace. *Journal of Vocational Behavior* 66(3), 438–456.

Hewlett, S. A. et al. (2017, July). People Suffer at Work When They Can't Discuss the Racial Bias They Face Outside of It. *Harvard Business Review*. https://hbr.org/2017/07/people-suffer-at-work-when-they-cant-discuss-the-racial-bias-they-face-outside-of-it [Last accessed 24 July 2021].

Iacobucci, G. (2020). Covid-19: Racism May Be Linked to Ethnic Minorities' Raised Death Risk, Says PHE. *British Medical Journal* 369, m2421.

Johnson, S. K., & Hekman, D. R. (2017). Women and Minorities Are Penalized for Promoting Diversity. *Harvard Business Review*. https://hbr.org/2016/03/women-and-minorities-are-penalized-for-promoting-diversity [Last accessed 24 July 2021].

Johnson, V. E., Nadal, K. L., Sissoko, D. G., & King, R. (2021). "It's Not in Your Head": Gaslighting, 'Splaining, Victim Blaming, and Other Harmful Reactions to Microaggressions. *Perspectives on Psychological Science* 16(5), 1024–1036.

Kiffin-Petersen, S. A. (2018). Ashamed of Your Shame? How Discrepancy Self-Talk and Social Discourse Influence Individual Shame at Work. In *Social Functions of Emotion and Talking about Emotion at Work*. Cheltenham, UK and Northampton, MA, USA: Edward Elgar Publishing.

Lorde, A. (2018). Microaggressions, Macroaggressions, and Modern Racism in the Workplace. *Microaggressions and Modern Racism: Endurance and Evolution* 105.

Milner, IV, H. R. (2007). Race, Culture, and Researcher Positionality: Working through Dangers Seen, Unseen, and Unforeseen. *Educational Researcher* 36(7), 388–400.

Sue, D. W., Alsaidi, S., Awad, M. N., Glaeser, E., Calle, C. Z., & Mendez, N. (2019). Disarming Racial Microaggressions: Microintervention Strategies for Targets, White Allies, and Bystanders. *American Psychologist* 74(1), 128.

Sue, D. W., & Spanierman, L. (2020). *Microaggressions in Everyday Life*. Hoboken, NJ: John Wiley & Sons.

Williams, M. T. (2021). Racial Microaggressions: Critical Questions, State of the Science, and New Directions. *Perspectives on Psychological Science* 16(5), 880–885.

7

"YOU HAVE SUCH A LOVELY, WELCOMING SMILE"

This chapter

- *describes the third of the three Model Black behaviours: softening,*
- *compares the differing amounts of effort softening demands from the Model Black,*
- *discusses the high levels of EQ found in the black male interviewees and*
- *considers how the Model Black trope limits black leaders.*

But you can't be too masculine; it doesn't work to be too masculine. You can't be that – you just won't be taken seriously. You definitely won't be promoted. It's so hard. I know so very few black guys in recruitment. The ones I know, they're good, but they're softly spoken. You have to be a certain type.

Naomi, Senior Recruitment Consultant

I'm not going to stand up and start shouting in the room because *I* want to be here. That's the thing. If I did start doing those types of things, I would be viewed differently than my white male colleagues who get upset, who curse, who do whatever when something doesn't go their way. I don't have that luxury to do that.

Anon, Senior Executive, Manufacturing

It only matters that black people are appointed if you bring yourself to work. Learn to get really comfortable in your own clothing, in your own shoes, because everybody else's is taken.

Grace Ononigu, CBE Director,
Crown Prosecution Services

DOI: 10.4324/9781003200482-11

You want to be able to show what you can do, but you also know it might create [negative] reactions from other colleagues that are just not helpful or even kind. When I was at the middle stage of my career, I experienced that quite a lot.

Anon, Board Member, IT

To the end of my service, there probably wasn't a week that went by when people didn't say, "Oh my gosh, you're not like the others. Oh my gosh."

Anon, Senior Officer, Public Service

SOFTENING AND THE MODEL BLACK

Although the Model Black uses squaring to avoid being perceived as "too black" and self-silencing to avoid raising concerns that could offend others and harm the way they are perceived, they may have still not have done enough to be "exemplary" in the eyes of white colleagues. So, they must ensure there are no remaining rough edges. I describe this as "softening." For many of them, softening is part of their personality, their natural leadership style. For others, it is something they have to think about and develop.

Softening is about being less of something, reducing something. It makes sense because the behaviours result in the Model Black leaders adopting certain leadership styles. Based on research from Hay/McBer, Goleman[1] describes six effective leadership styles: *Coercive* leaders demand immediate compliance,

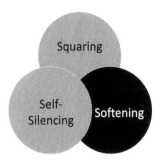

Figure 7.1 Softening

commanding others to do as they are told; *pacesetting* leaders expect excellence and self-direction, demanding quick results; *authoritative* leaders mobilise people toward a vision, inviting them to come with them; *affiliative* leaders create emotional bonds and harmony through empathy and building relationships; *democratic* leaders build consensus through participation; and *coaching* leaders develop people for the future through empathy and self-awareness. The majority of the black male leaders in this study talked about using styles that were affiliative, coaching or democratic. This means the black male leaders were not adopting styles that required them to command others or make strong demands on them. It was an inclusive style that had them working alongside their colleagues rather than leading from the front. It meant not openly competing with their colleagues. They knew they were better than their colleagues because they would otherwise not be in that role. However, they were not allowed to be arrogant or showy. This behaviour may have been their natural style. However, to what extent might this have been the only style that they were permitted to use amongst their white colleagues?

Through softening, Model Black leaders in this study play down aspects of their behaviour. The black men play down their masculinity. Black women, however, play down showing their emotions. Black men and women take care not to appear too confident or too intelligent. These aspects of their leadership style are important ways of avoiding the stereotypes associated with the tropes discussed in Chapter 5. There was evidence that these acts of softening may become less necessary for leaders once they reach the very top of their professions. However, they are an important success ingredient whilst they are still on their way up.

One black male leader talked about going through his profession being conscious that he was wearing a velvet glove. This was symbolic of the ways in which he mollified his behaviour. He would try hard to ensure that he never formed a fist in the glove. If he did ever make a fist, then he would punch extremely gently. He would never use an authoritative or pacesetting style. This awareness and behaviour were borne out of the knowledge that he was working against stereotypes that are different from those of his white and South and East Asian colleagues. The research for this book identified four types of softening as shown in Figure 7.2.

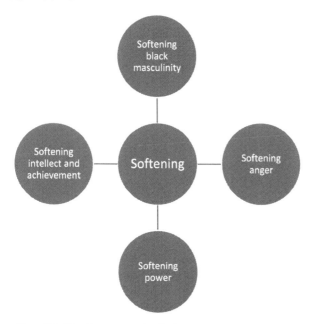

Figure 7.2 The four types of softening

SOFTENING BLACK MASCULINITY

The popular stereotypes of black men and boys, and the trope of the threatening black male body (as discussed in Chapters 2 and 4), are some distance from the image of the senior executive in a global corporation. However, awareness of these stereotypes can place a lot of stress on the daily actions of black men in the workplace. The black men I spoke to had to consider how simply being a black man affected the response they got from some colleagues. They noticed how some colleagues avoided eye contact or shifted uncomfortably in their seats. The black leaders introduced behaviours to help their colleagues; two of the men talked about lowering the tone of their voice. Two other men who described themselves as mixed-race suggested that they had some softening advantages over those with darker complexions. They recognised that they were perceived as the more acceptable shade of black, as long as they did not draw too much attention to their blackness.

In the interviews, I was struck by the sensitivity, affability and geniality of all of the black men I interviewed. They smiled easily and struck me as very even-tempered. This may have been a reflection of the sample, but I was left wondering whether this attribute is an essential trait for black men who want to succeed in a white environment. Maybe it is the case that assertive or arrogant black men did not make it to the top in white organisations?

I met Ken (pseudonym) at a senior leadership development event in Spain. In fact, I heard him before I met him. I was sitting waiting for a group of participants, and I heard a deep, loud laugh. However, the laughter went on for quite some time. It was as if he was laughing at every other comment that was being said by the crowd of people that he was approaching with. As he entered the room, I noticed he was a six-foot, four-inch, bald, dark black guy who probably weighed around 18 stone. There was something about his tendency to laugh that felt out of kilter with the moment. Was every comment really so funny? I noticed how amongst all the chatter from his colleagues, he laughed a lot more. I noticed that as the days went on, he was less jovial. It was as if he had settled into the new crowd. However, his permanent smile never left him. He was extremely polite and always spoke in a very calm and measured way. I was keen to interview him for this book. Had he always been this way, or was he consciously thinking about how to navigate his way as a large black man in a senior leadership role? When I interviewed him, he was warm, reflective and very self-aware. He was born in Nigeria to black professionals. He had a positive sense of self and was well grounded in his black culture and history. I immediately put him into the "Deserver" category. He told me about the weight he feels as one of the most senior black men in a successful global organisation. In many ways, he is like his white peers; he was privately educated, and he plays rugby and speaks in immaculate Queen's English. However, he was acutely aware that there is a high chance that he is the closest some of his colleagues have ever been to a black person. Ken felt as though their perception of the entire race was dependent on the experience they had with him. This affects the way he behaves. He told me about a conversation with a senior white executive:

> We have Ken in the team, and that was very good. So, now we'll hire two more black people. I thought to myself, "It's like

saying, 'I buy a Kenwood blender it's really great, so I buy two more Kenwood appliances.'" That's the reality. That you are representative of something where people are trying to form an impression, form a judgment. You represent something beyond you in a way that white people in the organisation do not.

Ken's jovial persona offered a softened version of black masculinity which worked well in the majority-white workplace.

Ken was also demonstrating a high level of emotional intelligence or EQ. As discussed in Chapter 4, research indicates that high levels of EQ result in higher-than-average performance.[2] Goleman[3] suggests that emotional intelligence encompasses four basic elements: self-awareness, self-management, social awareness and social skills. Self-awareness is about leaders being emotionally self-aware managers and being able to sense their emotional feelings anytime. Self-management concerns regulating or minimising destructive feelings or thoughts before taking action; social awareness is about empathy – considering the feelings of others before making decisions. Social skills are about the way leaders deal with issues, using teamwork, transparency and accountability, typically trying to find win–win solutions. I perceived a strong EQ evident in 80 per cent of the black men in this study.

THE SENSITIVITY QUOTIENT (SQ)

I reflected on whether these high levels of EQ amongst black men were the result of regular SCANing or whether their ability to SCAN effectively was a result of their high EQ? Either way, I felt that this was more than EQ; this was what I call the black man sensitivity quotient (SQ).

SQ is an essential ingredient for black male leaders as they navigate their white world. Black males need to be emotionally intelligent in ways that are not typically demanded from their white male counterparts. One reason for this is that if they make mistakes, then the climate is much less forgiving.

A key outcome of SQ is the ability to understand what the right leadership style for the right moment is. Leadership styles range from dictatorial to laissez-faire. In my experience as a leadership educator and coach, I have worked with white male leaders who exhibit every style across that spectrum. It was interesting, therefore, that 80 per cent of the black men I spoke to also described themselves as "collaborative" or "inclusive." This was also evident in my conversation with Chris Forbes. Chris has a senior role in a global consultancy; he talked about being a "we" guy. He talked about being happy to be the sheepdog and "leading from behind." This was also the case when dealing with clients. Although in a client-facing selling and consultancy role, Chris had a style that he describes as self-deprecating. Chris talked about being in client meetings where he felt that he was able to get along with them because they did not feel threatened by him. He would be more open to being corrected than his white colleagues and ready to admit to not being perfect. Rather than disagree, one of his standard responses was, "I think you've got a point there." Chris was clear that this was a choice he was making:

> I won't call it an insecurity, I'd frankly call it modesty perhaps if you like in that I'm happy to be corrected, too often some people say I am more than happy to point out my weaknesses or frailties, but I feel that people appreciate that quality and it's not just something that I'm doing for the sake of it.

I could appreciate why he was the type of black guy that people would feel comfortable around. He had told me about a role many years prior, where he had been referred to as "Chalkie." He had been happy to go along with this racially motivated nickname for many years. It had made no difference to his performance and meant that he was accepted by his team. Whilst it irritated him occasionally, he chose not to make it an issue, as this would mean asserting himself in a way that would not be good for his personal brand within the organisation.

I am curious as to whether the black men I spoke to would feel the need to exhibit the same levels of SQ if they worked within a primarily black organisation. I am left with the question of whether these men typically have an affiliative and collaborative nature and therefore get on well in the organisations or whether they have to work much harder at this in order to be accepted as black men?

Is one of the reasons that black men have this softer style also connected to concerns they may have around perceptions of their sexuality in the workplace? The idea of black men as sexual creatures and even sexual predators transfers from the broader society into the workplace. Black leaders were very aware of their sexuality in the workplace. Sir Trevor Phillips, CBE, former head of the Equalities Commission, told me how when he came to the UK, one of the key pieces of advice he was given by his mother was never to be alone in a room with a white woman, and if he had to be, then he should leave the door open! This motherly advice was motivated by concern for his safety in an all-white environment.

If it is the case that only the black man with a very high SQ gets on in organisations, then this raises a number of questions. Why is it that this standard is very different from what is expected from white males? To what extent are organisations losing out because they are not pulling from a more diverse pool of black men?

SOFTENING ANGER

Susannah (pseudonym) has been working alongside her new peer for three months. They have both attended elite universities, and both aspire to better things within the organisation. Her colleague is a middle-class white woman. She has a tendency to be bossy and condescending not only towards Susannah but the whole team. On one particular project, they disagree on the process they will use to achieve a set of outputs required by their joint manager at the end of the week. Susannah decides to focus on the outcomes and ignore the process, as this was what their manager had said they should prioritise. Her colleague is unhappy that the process she has designed has been ignored. They meet to talk about it. Susannah is calm. As they discuss, her colleague raises her voice and loses her composure as she demands to know why the process had not been followed. Susannah explains that she had to make a choice between the output and the process. She notes that whereas she had achieved her outputs, her colleague had not. Her colleague becomes visibly angrier, "I am very concerned with your attitude," she screams. Susannah would love to raise her voice just a little, or even match the tempo of her white colleague. She is momentarily conflicted. She SCANs. Should she match the energy of her white colleague and explain her position? Should she assert her opinion that there is more than one way to approach this task? As the Model Black, she knows that black women cannot get angry in the workplace. So, she does not respond. A black woman's anger conflicts with the mammy trope – and feeds the angry black woman trope (see Chapter 4).

The angry black woman, described by Judd[4] as "hands on hips, rolling eyes, wagging finger," is a trope that originated in the US. This trope has its origins in 19th-century America when white men dressed up as fat, angry black women. Later it became associated with the character "Sapphire," a character from a US radio show who was angry and irrational. So, this became the image of the black woman that Americans saw and internalised – she is angry at everyone around her, including the government and life in general. Sapphire is a person who wants to dominate. She is sensitive to injustice and likes to complain. She criticises for the sake of criticising rather than to improve things. This oversensitive angry black woman trope exists in broader society and consequently finds itself in the world of work. This trope is damaging because it trivialises the often-legitimate complaints of injustice made by black women.

This trope has crossed the Atlantic, and, in the UK, it can stop black women from being heard because the perception of who they are has already spoken for them. Hill-Collins[5] talks about the power of controlling images of black women, which are designed to oppress them. In this moment, Susannah was being controlled by the image of the angry black woman, unable to respond or answer back because she could be perceived as aggressive and threatening. What Susannah experienced was what Jones and Norwood[6] describe as "the complexity of that fleeting moment when Black women must decide whether and how to challenge another's assumptions." In this case, these are assumptions about black women's position in the workplace. The Model Black does not take this risk at work.

Julie offered another example of how a black woman has to weigh up the risk of being labelled as angry when confronted by a white person's anger. She told me about a virtual encounter with her CEO. Each week the managing directors would meet with the CEO to report on the week's activities. It would typically be a challenging environment where the CEO would seek to understand some of the detail of the business.

"No word of a lie, Barbara," Julie shared, "he started shouting at me . . . shouting on a conference call! He started shouting at me down the line. I'm sitting there, in front of all my colleagues, and I'm really angry, but I thought, 'Okay. I'm with my peers; I'm the only black person, I'm the only female, do I argue and play to what they would expect or do I hold back, get my facts together, and then come back?' I had to sit down and really take this guy shouting at me in this meeting with my peers, and in the end, I said, 'Do you know what? I'll come back to you.' It took a lot for me to do that. It took a hell of a lot for me to do that." Julie had never seen her boss behave in this way towards her white colleagues. Was it because she was black? Was it because she was a woman? Maybe he had simply woken up on the wrong side of the bed. Whatever the reason, the behaviour was unacceptable and unprofessional.

The Model Black man also avoids getting angry in the workplace. The societal perception of the angry black man is someone to be tasered, locked up and medicated. However, when I use the word "angry" here, it refers to the way that men are perceived by their white colleagues. A small degree of assertiveness can be perceived as anger when exhibited by black men. Why was it that I had not encountered any angry black men as I sought to find the black men who had successfully navigated their white workspaces? Maybe it is as simple as black men who show anger do not rise to the top of organisations. These men are weeded out early on when it is clear that they do not fit the ideal of black leadership. Perhaps the so-called angry black man cannot co-exist with white ideals of leadership.

I spoke with two black men who had felt unable to adopt the behaviour of the Model Black as it related to their behaviour at work. One now worked independently. He recognised that he could not become what was required for him to succeed in a corporate environment. If he was not able to match the energy he saw in his white colleagues, then he could not stay. If he could not express his emotions, then he could not be sufficiently productive at work. Research shows that individuals are more productive in environments where they are able to express more of themselves. So why should he not be allowed to show his feelings? Indeed, he suggested, not being allowed to show any degree of anger at any point in your career demands a lot from any individual. It demands more from you when you are met by anger, from other colleagues and outside work by the police and the judiciary.

I am not proposing that we have workplaces where anger is allowed to be expressed in a ubiquitous and uncontrolled way.

However, expecting behaviour from one section of the population which is not imposed on another seems extremely unfair and inequitable. This may be a key area where uncovering individual biases could be particularly helpful in promoting greater inclusion.

SOFTENING POWER

A US leader told me about an encounter he had had with a colleague. He was with his team at a very nice restaurant in New York, a Michelin two-star restaurant. It was when Barack Obama was running for president. The junior partner said at the table, "Do you think Barack is going to win? Yes or no. Why?" Everyone started throwing in their comments. He says, "I don't think he'll win the election. I support him, but he won't win it because he's an uppity nigger." The idea of a black person being "uppity" emerged in the US South as black people fought against discriminatory practices. The "uppity negro," a more commonly used term, dared to challenge society's racial norms. He was the fearless black person who was not prepared to stay "in his place." The UK does not have the same history with regards to the use of the term. However, the concept of the black leader who does not know their place is alive and kicking in the British workplace, and the Model Black know they have to navigate this phenomenon.

Things are more subtle in the British workplace. Cultural language is often used to demean black people who rise above their station. They tend to take the form of microaggressions, which, according to Sue, are the "brief and commonplace daily verbal, behavioural, and environmental indignities, whether intentional or unintentional, that communicate hostile, derogatory, or negative slights and insults to marginalized individuals and groups."[7] In the UK the uppity "black negro" is rearticulated in the black person who questions issues of power in relation to culture, attitude or competence. If the black British leader is seen to be behaving above their station, then they are put in their place often through their competence being challenged.

David Lammy, MP, told me about his competence being challenged when in government:

> When you are in a huge department, like the Ministry of Justice or the Education Department, you're the only black person

there. You're meant to be the Minister getting civil servants to do what you ask them to do, and you can see some of them questioning your right to do that, your legitimacy, whether you know what you're doing.

This questioning can also be more carefully worded. One leader explained that the comments made to him were subtle but different from those made to his white colleagues. He was the one who was asked, repeatedly asked, "Are you sure you understand?" Questions about attitudes towards work, as discussed in the example with Susannah, were also common.

Words are also used to describe individuals also cast aspersions on their competence and prevent them from being "uppity." Paul Cleal, OBE, talked about the adjectives used to describe him at PwC. The phrase "laid-back" was language that was only used to describe him. This language was imbued with the idea that he was lazy. White colleagues with similar temperaments may have been described as "calm under pressure." He suggests that it is within those telltale phrases and words that people often use to describe you that you can see the ways in which the subtleties of language play out. "To describe a black person as 'laid-back,' which kind of implies they're not really bothered either way, and people interpret your behaviour in that sort of manner and see what they would see in a white person as very positive, calm, unflappable and portray it as negative. So the connotation is that he may be 'a bit lazy,' and maybe, 'isn't probably really that bothered.' You have to deal with those sorts of things. The danger is that some people are able to see through this use of language, but some are not. There are people in organisations who are projecting their biased views onto others."

SOFTENING INTELLECT AND ACHIEVEMENT

The Model Black is aware of the dangers of being over-competent or super intelligent. Around a quarter of those I interviewed talked about learning how to be successful without "bigging themselves up" too much, recognising the threat that their colour may represent; they are concerned that any kind of hubristic show could be damaging to others' perception of them. Whilst they did not actively downplay their achievements, they were especially careful about not appearing overconfident or arrogant. For example, one leader was responsible for the largest client account in the organisation. She worked hard to keep it, and the client was delighted but never mentioned this fact in internal meetings. Yet, she was constantly faced with white colleagues playing on their achievements in public. She recognised that the potential downside of this was that some might not know of her achievements. However, she calculated that this was outweighed by the lack of attention that was placed on her. Whereas women have a tendency to downplay their achievements,[8] this comment was heard from both black men and women in this study.

Five of the black leaders learnt how to succeed despite not feeling able to actively demonstrate their full intelligence at work. They were cautious because they felt that they might be perceived as threatening to their colleagues. They had observed a kind of fragility in their senior white colleagues and so worked out at what stage they should offer up their full knowledge. One leader talked of this being especially common when there was a third party present. Naomi told me, "I play down my intelligence at work a lot. Where I do use my intelligence, it is with my clients or with my candidates." She had found that she could shine in client meetings away from the organisation. She also felt that she had a particular talent when it came to preparing senior candidates for their roles. Her expertise in this area resulted in higher-than-average placements. However, it meant that her relationships with colleagues were protected. Patricia Miller, OBE, also talked about times before she became chief executive in the NHS when she felt unable to say what she thought. Her strategy was to make an appointment to speak to somebody quite senior. For her getting the right outcome was more important than her being the driving force behind it.

This raises questions about whether organisations are getting the best out of their black leaders. Concerns around being too intelligent can mean that great ideas are not voiced, and potential solutions are missed. It is a key risk of diversity in the absence of inclusion.

THE MODEL BLACK MATTERS

The Model Black comprises a collection of characteristics that are required for black leaders to navigate white workplaces. These are the nine elements in the profile of the Model Black discussed in Chapter 4. In addition, there are the three behaviours of squaring, self-silencing and softening. The combination of the profile and the behaviours enables black leaders to win at a game that was not designed for them to play. None of the black leaders I spoke to do all the things that would make them a Model Black. All of them did many of them.

Black leaders are no more a homogenous group than white leaders. What unites them is the challenges they face on account of their race. Each leader will have their individual way of expressing their profile and the three behaviours. There is no single recipe for success that can be followed by all black leaders.

The Model Black is a response to the expectations of white colleagues of what it means to be a leader. White leaders are evaluated as more effective and having more leadership potential than black leaders.[9] So black leaders start at a disadvantage because of the negative stereotypes that are associated with their race. This means they are often on their guard, ensuring that they do not make the wrong impression. They start out on the backfoot, run faster to get to the top and then have to put in extra effort to stay there. Those who succeed regard themselves as resilient fighters, not victims of a system.

The Model Black is both a conformity and a constraint. It limits the repertoire of responses for black leaders. For many, it means that there are elements of their true self that they cannot bring to work. In addition, this process of conforming demands mental energy – whether at a conscious or a subconscious level.

The Model Black would benefit from white colleagues who are cognisant of the issues that black leaders face. Colleagues who truly want to understand before they seek to act. Paulo Friere[10] talks about the notion of "conscientisation," which is about individuals understanding behaviours and systems to get an in-depth understanding of what is going then reflecting and taking action to reduce injustice. Through conscientisation, these white colleagues can make better decisions around the recruitment and promotion of black leaders; they can create a climate where there is space for black leaders to bring more of themselves to work. Maybe the conscientised white leader could create a climate where the Model Black becomes a choice rather than a necessity. This would mean having diverse types of black people in the organisation and not just those who fit the Model Black.

KEY TAKEAWAYS

- Softening is about playing down aspects to smooth any remaining rough edges to make white colleagues comfortable.
- For many black male leaders, softening was part of their natural leadership style; they typically had leadership styles that were affiliative and democratic.
- The Model Black is not necessarily a choice but a response to the organisational cultures in which black leaders find themselves.
- Understanding the new trope of Model Black is an essential starting point for creating more inclusive cultures.

QUESTIONS FOR REFLECTION

- Are there aspects of yourself that you work hard to soften in the workplace?
- What impact do you think softening has on black leaders?
- How can you create an environment where all your colleagues feel free to bring more of themselves to work?

NOTES

1 Goleman, D. (2000, March–April). Leadership That Gets Results. *Harvard Business Review*. https://hbr.org/2000/03/leadership-that-gets-results [Last accessed 23 July 2021].

2 Goleman, D. (2004). *Emotional Intelligence: Why It Can Matter More Than IQ & Working with Emotional Intelligence*. London: Bloomsbury.

3 Goleman, D. (2004). *Emotional Intelligence: Why It Can Matter More Than IQ & Working with Emotional Intelligence*. London: Bloomsbury.

4 Judd, B. (2019). Sapphire as Praxis: Toward a Methodology of Anger. *Feminist Studies* 45(1), 178–208. www.jstor.org/stable/10.15767/feminist-studies.45.1.0178 [Last accessed 5 May 2021].

5 Collins, P. H. (2002). *Black Feminist Thought: Knowledge, Consciousness, and the Politics of Empowerment*. New York: Routledge.

6 Jones, T., & Norwood, K. J. (2017). Aggressive Encounters & White Fragility: Deconstructing the Trope of the Angry Black Woman. *Iowa Law Review* 102(5).

7 Sue, D. W., & Spanierman, L. (2020). *Microaggressions in Everyday Life*. Hoboken, NJ: John Wiley & Sons.

8 Exley, C. L., & Kessler, J. B. (2019). *The Gender Gap in Self-Promotion (No. w26345).* Cambridge, MA: National Bureau of Economic Research.

9 Rosette, A. S. et al. (2008). The White Standard: Racial Bias in Leader Categorization. *Journal of Applied Psychology* 93(4), 758–777. https://doi.org/10.1037/0021-9010.93.4.758.

10 Freire, P. (2000). Cultural Action for Freedom. Revisited Edition. *Harvard Educational Review: Monograph Series* 1.

REFERENCES AND ADDITIONAL READING

Beyer, S. (1990). Gender Differences in the Accuracy of Self-Evaluations of Performance. *Journal of Personality and Social Psychology* 59(5), 960.

Budworth, M. H., & Mann, S. L. (2010). Becoming a Leader: The Challenge of Modesty for Women. *Journal of Management Development* 29, 177–186.

Clance, P. R., & Imes, S. A. (1978). The Imposter Phenomenon in High Achieving Women: Dynamics and Therapeutic Intervention. *Psychotherapy: Theory, Research & Practice* 15(3), 241.

Collins, P. H. (1986). Learning from the Outsider Within: The Sociological Significance of Black Feminist Thought. *Social Problems* 33(6), s14–s32.

Collins, P. H. (2002). *Black Feminist Thought: Knowledge, Consciousness, and the Politics of Empowerment.* New York. Routledge.

Crenshaw, K. W. (2018). Beyond Racism and Misogyny: Black Feminism and 2 Live Crew. In J. Matsuda, (Ed.), *Words That Wound: Critical Race Theory, Assaultive Apeech, and the First Amendment* (pp. 111–132). New York, London: Routledge.

Exley, C. L., & Kessler, J. B. (2019). The gender gap in self-promotion (No. w26345). National Bureau of Economic Research.

Freire, P. (2000). Cultural Action for Freedom (Revisited Edition). *Harvard Educational Review. Monograph Series* (1).

Gilbert, D. (2005, January 1). Interrogating Mixed-Race: A Crisis of Ambiguity? *Social Identities* 11(1), 55–74.

Goleman, D. (2000, March–April). Leadership that Gets Results. *Harvard Business Review.* https://hbr.org/2000/03/leadership-that-gets-results [Last accessed 23 July 2021].

Goleman, D. (2004). *Emotional Intelligence: Why It Can Matter More than IQ & Working with Emotional Intelligence.* London: Bloomsbury.

Harris, K. M. (2012). Burden of the Beautiful Beast: Visualization and the Black Male Body. *Contemporary Black American Cinema: Race, Gender and Sexuality at the Movies* 40–55.

Jackson, C. (2011). *Violence, Visual Culture, and the Black Male Body.* New York, London: Routledge.

Jones, T., & Norwood, K. J. (2017). Aggressive Encounters & White Fragility: Deconstructing the Trope of the Angry Black Woman. *Iowa Law Review* 102(5).

Joseph-Salisbury, R., Connelly, L., & Wangari-Jones, P. (2020). "The UK Is Not Innocent": Black Lives Matter, Policing and Abolition in the UK. *Equality, Diversity and Inclusion: An International Journal* 40(1), 21–28.

Judd, B. (2019). Sapphire as Praxis: Toward a Methodology of Anger. *Feminist Studies* 45(1), 178–208. www.jstor.org/stable/10.15767/feminist-studies.45.1.0178 [Last accessed 5 May 2021].

Krosch, A. R., Berntsen, L., Amodio, D. M., Jost, J. T., & Van Bavel, J. J. (2013). On the Ideology of Hypodescent: Political Conservatism Predicts Categorization of Racially Ambiguous Faces as Black. *Journal of Experimental Social Psychology* 49(6), 1196–1203.

Lenney, E. (1977). Women's Self-Confidence in Achievement Settings. *Psychological Bulletin* 84(1), 1.

Metzl, J. M. (2010). *The Protest Psychosis: How Schizophrenia Became a Black Disease.* Boston: Beacon Press

Rhode, D. L. (2017). *Women and Leadership.* New York: Oxford University Press.

Rosette, A. S. et al. (2008). The White Standard: Racial Bias in Leader Categorization. *Journal of Applied Psychology* 93(4), 758–777. https://doi.org/10.1037/0021-9010.93.4.758.

Sabat, I. E. et al. (2020). Stigma Expression Outcomes and Boundary Conditions: A Meta-Analysis. *Journal of Business and Psychology* 35, 171–186. https://doi.org/10.1007/s10869-018-9608-z

Selzer, L. F. (2010). Barack Obama, the 2008 Presidential Election, and the New Cosmopolitanism: Figuring the Black Body. *Melus* 35(4), 15–37.

Smith, E. L. B., & Nkomo, S. M. (2003). *Our Separate Ways: Black and White Women and the Struggle for Professional Identity.* Boston, Massachusetts: Harvard Business Press.

Sue, D. W., & Spanierman, L. (2020). *Microaggressions in Everyday Life.* Hoboken, NJ: John Wiley & Sons.

Woldemikael, E., & Woldemikael, O. (2021, March). From Suits to Royals: The Politics of Meghan Markle's Racial Ambiguity. *Women's Studies International Forum* 85, 102439.

SECTION 3

HOW WE WILL GET THERE

8

"TREAT ME THE SAME; VALUE MY DIFFERENCE"

This chapter

- *highlights the six actions an individual can take to improve inclusion in the workplace,*
- *describes a framework for how non-black individuals should deal with racism in the moment and*
- *argues the need for leaders to experience a consequential transition if they are to become truly inclusive.*

I don't want to be the mouthpiece to all my white colleagues to educate them on everything. What I can do is tell them about what's happened to us and what they can do to make it easier, but I don't want to be, "You need to do this, this, and this."

Derek Bruce, Head of Leadership
Development, Signify

Use your power. Particularly if you're male, upper class and white. Don't give me this bullshit around meritocracy, because I've met so many white men, upper-middle-class men, who have no idea they didn't get there on merit. They got there because their dad knew someone. They knew someone. They got a leg up because they went to a certain kind of school.

David Lammy, MP

DOI: 10.4324/9781003200482-13

You can't say "I'm not racist because I have a black friend." Get to know that black person, be curious about that particular person that you're dealing with, and know them.

Irene Poku, Former Senior Scientist, Pharmaceuticals

When organisations select a leader, they should explore diversity with them as part of the recruitment process. If you're going to lead an organisation, why would you not talk to that leader about, or examine, their biases?

Lorna Matty, People Development Manager, Toyota

I said to people in the National Health Service, "I can provide some guidance on what needs to change, but the power to change it sits with our white communities, and it's about them seeing whiteness differently." That's the biggest message I think they need to hear is the solution actually sits with them. We can advise, but they need to do the work. Until that starts to happen, nothing will change.

Patricia Miller, OBE, Chief Executive Officer, NHS

We [black leaders] are not saying you're lost, and you can't be found. We're saying you are an intelligent person; you do stuff – maybe with good intentions, and maybe you don't have any intentions behind it at all, but we want you to understand that this is how it comes across, and this is what you could do.

Anon, Executive, Financial Services

WORKING IT OUT WITH CARRY

My close friend is Carry, a Dutch executive coach. She is a kind, amiable white woman with whom I can share my personal and professional challenges. Over our many conversations, I became interested in her life in the Netherlands, and Carry was genuinely curious about my black British life. In 2011, I was teaching on an executive programme in early December, shortly before "Sinterklaas evening." This is the evening when St Nicholas brings gifts for Dutch children. It is a long-standing Dutch tradition that dates back hundreds of years. I knew relatively little about this tradition, other than we always had to finish early if we ever ran an executive education programme on that day. On this particular occasion, Carry brought me gifts and sweets to celebrate. The chocolates looked particularly delectable, wrapped in colourful packaging. It was clear that she had gone to some effort and expense. On the packaging, there were images of a black person. It looked to me like a cross between the gollywog I saw on jam jars when growing up and a black Santa. I inquired into who this was. Carry explained that it was Black Piet (Zwarte Piet in Dutch), Saint Nicolas's companion and helper. I asked why he was black, and my friend politely explained that it was because he had come through the chimney and was, therefore, covered in soot. I do not recall my exact response; however, Carry recalls it vividly. She says that I told her calmly and politely that it was ridiculous to suggest that this was a white person covered in soot and that I was surprised that black people in the Netherlands did not take offence at this clearly negative stereotype. At best, it looked like a black person in a subordinate position. At worst, it resembled a white Santa with a black slave. I was confused that this should be a cause for celebration. Carry explained that she had friends from Surinam who partook in the "Sinterklaas evening" celebrations and never mentioned anything about being offended. Sinterklaas was an established Dutch tradition that went back many years and was not designed to harm anyone.

I asked Carry about this recently, and she explained that she felt extremely uncomfortable by my response. She can still recall the emotions of shock, anxiety, confusion and guilt that she experienced in that moment. Shock, because this was totally unexpected.

"I was shocked at watching you being shocked," Carry recalled to me later. She felt an intense array of emotions: anxiety because she could not imagine that I could believe that she would intentionally bring something that would offend me, confusion because engrained in her mind was the thought that this was an innocent portrayal designed to cheer up children with no malicious intent and guilt because the chocolates, in particular, were supposed to offer me a positive image of this Dutch tradition and instead they had served to caused me concern and possibly offence. The event hurt Carry deeply, especially because of our close friendship.

As well as experiencing her own feelings, Carry was able to feel with me, to empathise. She was getting a sense of what it might be like to be on the receiving end of unintended and unconscious racist behaviour. We had further conversations where she worked at being in my space, trying to get a sense of what my life might be like. Maybe it was Carry's experience as a coach, but I had the sense that she was experiencing something transformative in the way that she understood and related to me as a black woman.

In the years since that interaction, the character of Black Piet has become increasingly controversial and become the subject of height- ened debate and controversy in the Netherlands.[1] Carry told me how when the debate took hold, she found her interaction with me very valuable in helping her understand the range of perspectives that were being put forward. She tried hard to put herself in the shoes of black Dutch people. Carry believes that our conversation and her memory of our emotions when I opened the gifts allowed her to take on board the alternative points of view.

"You showed me that the image might not be okay," she told me recently. After the event, Carry took some time to understand the origins of Black Piet. She understood the character was popularised in a mid-19th-century children's book written by a man interested in members of the Dutch royal family, one of whom had bought a slave in a slave market in Cairo in the mid-19th century. According to Joke Hermes,[2] professor of media, culture and citizenship at Inholland University, it is thought that this slave may have helped inspire the character of Zwarte Piet. The debate continues in the Netherlands, but by 2020, McDonald's had banned employees from dressing as Black Piet, and the Dutch police announced it no longer allows Black Piet costumes at its holiday parties.

I understood that my Dutch friend had been brought up in a society where, as part of a white majority, she had never thought about her colour. She had never contemplated the fact that she was racialised as white. Carry had no reason to notice that an image that struck me immediately as a negative racial stereotype could poten- tially offend. It was a reminder that racial tropes and stereotypes can be so engrained that the majority culture does not even think to talk about them, and black people do not feel comfortable raising them. I reflected further on the conversation I had with Carry. Our rela- tionship meant that we were able to discuss the issue openly and her sensitivity meant that she was able to notice the effect that being challenged in the area of race had on her. I admired her bravery in speaking out about the issue when it was raised later on and was encouraged by her desire to educate herself. I also recognised that Carry had opened herself up to being transformed in how she now thinks and speaks about racial issues as they relate to black people.

Carry's story points to some of the themes that emerged in conversation with black leaders regarding how to improve inclusion in the workplace; the importance of curiosity, building relationships, an understanding of white fragility and bias and an interest in education and becoming a true ally. However, it also spoke to something that I feel is missing in much of the education and training around race, the need to be prepared to transform the way you understand and approach issues of race.

HOW TO DO IT DIFFERENTLY: THE INDIVIDUAL LEVEL

In 2016, I enrolled for a master's in organisational change. One of the programme's basic tenets was that you could not work with organisations to help them bring about change unless you had first done work on yourself. Part of this work involved accepting what Gergen[3] calls a socially constructed position, recognising that there are alternative versions of knowledge and truth which are socially fabricated and maintained through social interaction. This approach recognised that my own constructed world is patterned and filtered, enabled and constrained by those with whom I spend my time. This was important work that allowed me to grow as an individual and as a consultant. I saw this development as a long-term journey rather than an achievable destination. I believe that this approach is important for developing inclusive leaders. During the programme, like Stacey,[4] I also came to realise that an organisation is not a "thing" but is made up of many individuals. What happens in organisations is not simply the outcome of choices made by powerful people in the organisation but is a consequence of local conversations and interactions of many people. This would suggest that to make an organisation more inclusive, it is necessary to have numerous leaders who recognise the knowledge and behaviours needed to bring about that change. So, where do we start?

Starting out is not about putting the responsibility solely on the shoulders of white leaders. The black leaders I spoke to want to play their part in establishing a culture of inclusion. They recognised that

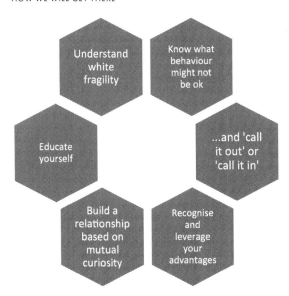

Figure 8.1 Individual actions to promote inclusion

a key step to achieving this is working with their white colleagues to promote and practice the right behaviours. The leaders I spoke to offered suggestions as to what could be done on an individual level, many of which reflected my personal experience with Carry (Figure 8.1).

Educate yourself

After our conversation, Carry chose to educate herself on the issue we were discussing. Two-thirds of the black leaders proposed that their white leaders take some time to educate themselves. Black leaders said they were happy to respond to genuine curiosity but did not want full responsibility for educating their white colleagues. As part of the non-dominant culture, black leaders are obliged to understand the dominant culture. They understand the history, the customs, the language. Sometimes it feels like it is happening by osmosis, and sometimes it takes additional effort. Those from the dominant culture have the luxury of not needing to understand the history or culture of other groups. However, this can mean that they come to interactions and conversations around race with a huge lack of knowledge. This ignorance can lead to a lack of progress in bringing about inclusion.

It seems appropriate to ask white professionals to take some time to do some online research, read some books and watch some films to get an insight into the daily experiences of others. Recognising that the lives and experiences of black people may be very different from their own is an important starting point. A wider understanding of black history and culture, especially as it relates to the black experience in the UK, is also needed. Black leaders can find it difficult to engage in conversations with white colleagues who have not done this basic work. The question non-black readers may be asking is, "Where do I start?" The answer is that there is a lot of accessible information on websites, blogs and podcasts. Why not start with *Brit(ish): On Race, Identity and Belonging* by Afua Hirsch[5] and *Black and British: A Forgotten History* by David Olusoga[6] (also available as a BBC series) and *The Windrush Betrayal: Exposing the Hostile Environment* by Amelia Gentleman.[7] For UK historical context, the BBC Small Axe films directed by Steve McQueen[8] offer excellent insights. For US texts, go to *How to Be an Antiracist* by Ibram X. Kendi[9] and for more extensive resources, see Cooley's[10] Allyship and Antiracism Resource Kit.

Part of this education should be to understand the language of race. Understand how your black colleagues want to be referred to. As discussed in Chapter 1, the term black can be a political term. It is, though, a term that black people of African and Caribbean origin are typically comfortable with. Ask your mixed-heritage leaders how they want to be referred to. Those I interviewed were comfortable with the term mixed-race. However, it is wrong to assume that all are. Some black people will want to be referred to by their place of origin, such as African or African Caribbean. Others prefer to include their specific countries of origin, like British-Nigerian, British-Ghanaian, Zambian or South African. If in doubt, ask.

Understand white fragility

In Chapter 4, I talked of the importance of black leaders knowing how to respond to what DiAngelo[11] refers to as white fragility.

White fragility results from a socialised sense of superiority that white people are either unaware of or cannot admit to themselves. It manifests itself as anger, fear and argumentation when their worldview as it relates to race and racism is challenged. The mention of racism is seen as a challenge to their identities as good people. DiAngelo suggests that this response is a powerful means of white racial control. The black leaders I spoke to did not use the language of racial control or white supremacy nor mention the term "white fragility." However, they wanted to encourage their white colleagues to be aware of the patterns of their own responses when discussing issues of race. One of the reasons for the self-silencing discussed in Chapter 6 was the anticipated defensive response from white colleagues. Half of the leaders talked about wanting to feel able to speak openly with their colleagues without being overly concerned about how they would respond. Black leaders understand that there will be disagreement and discussion on issues of difference and that we may not always share the same viewpoint. However, they ask that white people notice their response even if they cannot prevent it.

My friend Carry knew nothing of the term white fragility. However, she was able to notice the impact that my comments were having on her in that moment. This ability to notice prevented her from digging in and assertively defending her position. Recognising your emotions when the subject of race is discussed can be a helpful starting point. Knowing that anger and rejection may be your initial response can be the beginning of a process of understanding. This recognition of emotions can influence your response and result in a better personal connection and, ultimately, greater inclusion. The Model Black does not immediately associate unintentional racism with bad people. They know that good people say and do wrong things on occasion – just as they do! Carry is a good person who lacked the understanding that some of the things she takes for granted could be offensive to people of colour. Her lack of understanding of the historical context of Black Piet and the broader issues around negative black tropes and stereotypes meant that she was not initially able to have an informed conversation around the issue. Start by reading and reflecting on DiAngelo's book.

Recognise and leverage your advantages

There are many conditions that white leaders take for granted.[12] White leaders believe their voice will be heard in a group, even if they are the only white person there. They think that, even if they have low credibility as a leader, they can be sure that their race is not the problem. In white-dominated workplaces (for example, in the UK), white leaders have more of a sense that they belong than black leaders. They also know that an argument with a colleague of another race is more likely to jeopardise their chances for promotion than their own. They can be comfortable that they can be late to a meeting without having the lateness reflect on their race. The list goes on.

The notion of white privilege or "white advantage," as I prefer to call it, is based on the suggestion that white people have had certain advantages for centuries. The idea is that since colonial times, the world has been divided between the dominated (people of colour) and the dominating (whites). The result has been that this domination has afforded whites a set of insurmountable privileges that go beyond their individual class or power status.[13] An understanding of white advantage means white people seeing themselves as racialised as white and recognising the benefits that this gives them. Research on perceptions of race among white women in the early '90s in the US[14] surfaced how these women did not see themselves as "having a race" in the same way that men did not see themselves as having a gender. Race was invisible to them and gave them benefits, but it was not visible to others who were not like them.

This invisible advantage can be hard to face up to in the workplace. The idea that your achievements are not based solely on merit and that the organisation does not have a level playing field is tough to stomach. Twenty of the leaders talked about the importance of white leaders using their power to benefit others in the organisation. The black leaders wanted white male leaders, in particular, to use their power to support the understanding that racism is not a black problem but something that all employees need to understand and engage with.

You can start by playing a part in supporting under-represented groups. This could be through sponsoring black colleagues, recommending them for projects, telling them about development opportunities and offering practical support.

Build a relationship based on mutual curiosity

Twenty-two of the 30 leaders I spoke to talked about wanting their white colleagues to have a better understanding of who they are. One black senior leader I spoke to suggested that rather than attend an inclusive leadership course, his white colleagues should just hang out with black people for a couple of weeks! He stressed the importance of spending time with individuals who are different from you and approaching the experience with an open mind. When probed, the leader said that he wished his white colleagues would get to know him, build a real relationship that is based on genuine curiosity. By "curiosity," he meant a genuine desire to seek out new information, asking questions so that they can understand his world and the experiences that have shaped his beliefs.

Real curiosity also requires the suspension of judgement as you listen with a preparedness to have your perspective opened and altered. One of the leaders expressed the importance of letting go of the idea that having a conversation about the difference is either about "pushing" your point of view on the other or avoiding the conversation altogether. In her research on curiosity, Francesca Gino,[15] a Harvard Business School professor, found when we are able to hold onto our curiosity, or when our curiosity is triggered and fostered in us, we are much more likely to have networks that are quite diverse and more likely to show less bias. We may also be able to engage more positively in conversations that we thought might be difficult. These same conversations can even become more enjoyable.

One leader told me how the senior partner in a global services company took the three new black trainees in his team out to dinner at a restaurant in Tottenham, London. The partner had been educated at an elite private school and offered to take them out for dinner at a restaurant of their choice. Two of his trainees had been to London state schools, and a third black professional had attended a grammar school. Organising the dinner in which he was the only minority was already a daring new step for the partner. He wanted this to be a positive experience for all of them – getting to know new people in an environment that was less comfortable for him. By the end of the evening, each side had moved from seeing each other as a stereotype of what they expected someone from that background to be, to seeing each other as interesting colleagues. The trainees felt that this was a step towards them feeling more included. They had started to get to know each other as human beings – not solely as individuals from different backgrounds. However, the effort had to come from the white senior partner. He was also responsible for setting the mood for the evening and modelling the behaviour he was encouraging in his trainees. Organising this first step did not mean that there would be immediate openness and trust. However, it was a helpful step in the right direction. If he could continue to build trust and understanding in the team, said one of those present, then there could be space in the future for being honest about their experiences of being black in the organisation. This was an important move towards equity in that there was an understanding that something specific was required to bring a black group into the team. Importantly, such an event could not have been initiated by the trainees.

Know what behaviour might not be okay

I recall a conversation with an extremely pleasant client who had just returned from a holiday in South Africa. He was at pains to tell me, as a black woman, how relieved he was that black people in the UK are not as lazy as those he met in South Africa. As he mentioned this, his white colleagues looked, nodded in agreement and smiled politely. Kevin, who we met in Chapter 1, told me how a white female partner in his firm came to their black network event and announced that as a white working-class female with a northern accent, she related to their experience as black leaders. They, too, smiled politely! Black leaders are still told by their well-meaning colleagues that they do not see them as black. These three examples can be regarded as microaggressions.[16] These "everyday insults, indignities and demeaning messages sent to people of colour by well-intentioned white people who are unaware of the hidden messages being sent" can eat away at you over time. Many black people live these every day of their lives, whereas white people have the luxury of time to understand and master microaggressions. Three types of microaggressions have been identified by Derald Wing Sue[17] and his colleagues: microassaults, microinsults and microinvalidation.

Microassaults are conscious and deliberate slurs, such as using racial epithets, displaying swastikas or deliberately serving a white person before a black person in a restaurant. A microassault could also be referring to someone as "coloured." This kind of behaviour can be because a person believes privately that a black person is inferior and then publicly express this belief when they lose control or feel relatively safe.

A *microinsult* is verbal or non-verbal communication that demeans a person's racial heritage or identity. An example is an employee who asks a black colleague how she got her job, suggesting that she may have got it solely on account of her skin colour. In this kind of situation, the context is important. Microinsults can also be non-verbal when, for example, a white colleague seems distracted during a conversation with a black employee by avoiding eye contact or turning away.

A *microinvalidation* is a communication that subtly excludes, negates or nullifies a black person's thoughts, feelings or experiential reality. For instance, white people might ask a black British leader where they are from, conveying the message that they are foreigners in their own land. Equally, when black people are told, "I don't see colour," or "We are all human beings," this can reduce or diminish their experiences as racial/cultural beings. When a black couple is given poor service at a restaurant and shares their experience with white friends, only to be told, "Don't be so oversensitive," or "Don't be so petty," the racial experience of the couple is diminished. Understanding and avoiding microaggressions is an important step towards inclusion.

These three microaggressions matter because, as Williams[18] suggests, they represent more than simple cultural missteps or racial faux pas. They are a form of oppression that reinforce power differentials between groups. You can start by gaining a better understanding of microaggressions by reading the tables on pages 276 and 277 of Sue et al.'s 2007 paper "Racial Microaggressions in Everyday Life Implications for Clinical Practice."[19]

. . . and then "call it out" or "call it in"

"Maybe I have been unlucky, but I have never been in a situation where a white colleague has spoken up for me. When something inappropriate is said, there is silence or laughter, nothing in between." Sympathy and understanding are always welcomed. However, using your white advantage to comment on something that is not okay would be even better. Most of the black leaders agree that they did not want unpleasant behaviour to go unchallenged. There was an agreement that such challenges should be selective. Black leaders know that the stakes can be high when white people use their position to speak out on behalf of their black colleagues. However, the stakes are higher for a black person. Black leaders want white colleagues to be brave enough to question and challenge bad behaviour. They understand that this takes courage. However, if white leaders are not prepared to take that step, this behaviour can become normalised. At the heart of this is the difference between being "non-racist" – that is, not engaging in racist behaviour – and being an "antiracist" – someone who is challenging racist behaviour. This behaviour should be challenged whether or not there is a black person in the room.

"Calling out" and "calling in" are both about letting others know that their behaviour is not okay. "Calling out" is naming it in the moment, in front of whoever is there. "Calling in" is about doing it later, more personally and taking the time to explore the incident and explain why it was offensive. However, in both cases, the framing is important. If the context allows, then framing it as a learning opportunity can be beneficial.

If you do not feel comfortable raising an issue alone in the moment, then find others who share your perspective and raise it as a group.

Jonathan Akwue, a senior executive in advertising, told me that he often called out sexist behaviour in his team. Comments from other leaders indicated that those around them had greater comfort confronting issues of sexism or homophobia than racism.

STAY OPEN: CHALLENGING RACISM IN THE MOMENT

How do non-black people intervene? A useful intellectual start is to read Sue and colleagues'[20] 2019 paper "Disarming Racial Microaggressions: Microintervention Strategies for Targets, White Allies, and Bystanders." Then, take the five aforementioned actions.

Now you are ready to adopt the OPEN framework.

The OPEN framework is a way for white people, in particular, to consider how to respond in your daily interactions with black colleagues – the essential foundation for understanding what situations require a response. Specifically, the framework provides individuals with a set of questions to work through during interactions with black colleagues, particularly when these dealings do not appear to be going smoothly.

The first part of the framework is to OBSERVE. Notice carefully what is happening in the moment. What did my colleague/client/boss/friend just say or do? Then gain PERSPECTIVE. How does this connect to what I know about the black person's experience? How does it connect to what I have learnt about race? What makes me think/feel that this is not right? The third step is to ENGAGE. What should I do whilst still in this situation? Should I do nothing? Should I call it our now? Should I call it in later? Finally, what should I do NEXT? Do I approach my black colleague? Do I raise it with the white leader? Do I "make it formal?"

In the same way as black leaders SCAN, white leaders are invited to stay OPEN as they work with race in the moment.

In addition to the individual work outlined so far in this chapter, inclusive leadership training also plays a role.

DEVELOPING INCLUSIVE LEADERS

One of the delights of working in management education for over 20 years is seeing real change in the insights and behaviours of senior managers in organisations, being present for the "aha" moment when the leaders see their behaviours as others see them, hearing about the huge impact their changed leadership style has on their teams and those around them. I see these changes across the range of leadership development programmes that I have had the pleasure to work on. These changes extend to programmes on inclusive leadership.

I view inclusive leadership development as a natural extension of leadership training. Being inclusive is an essential aspect of being the best leader that you can be. It provides an additional string to the leadership bow that increases the repertoire of leadership awareness and behaviours. Working on inclusive leadership development programmes, I have had the pleasure of observing leaders extend their existing leadership understanding by doing deep work on their individual attitudes and beliefs towards inclusion and how this affects behaviour in their organisations. This deep development is effective on an individual level. However, it requires time to be spent in personal development sessions, one-to-one personal coaching and facilitated peer group learning over an extended period. Ironically, such personal development can require significant investment by the organisation, so it cannot be as inclusive as companies may wish.

Such leadership development programmes do not occur in a vacuum. Their impact is reliant on organisations allowing individuals to challenge their power structures. The impact of such training is reduced when leaders have to work in organisations with entrenched practices.

My previous research on how management education[21] connects with the workplace identified the challenges of newly trained managers returning to organisations. They often found that they could not act out their new behaviours in the context of their organisation's culture – for that, work must be done at the organisational level, too. We will discuss this in Chapter 10.

FROM "DOING" DIFFERENT TO "BEING" DIFFERENT

How do we move beyond the head nodding and superficial changes in inclusive behaviour to a deeper understanding? How do we make the shift from doing inclusion to being inclusive (Figure 8.2)?

The black leaders in this study wanted their white colleagues to work on the six areas outlined earlier as a precursor to conversations around race. However, black leaders recognised that adopting many of the behaviours represented a cosmetic change for a lot of their colleagues, and in many cases, the colleagues did not feel the behavioural changes were necessary. As one interviewee shared, "The white leaders attend the inclusion course and nod their heads. But later they'll say, 'Why are black people so oversensitive?'"

Consequential transitions

My experience of facilitating conversations and training over many years suggests that whilst there is cognitive learning, the shift from

Consequential Transition

Figure 8.2 Move from "doing inclusion" to "being" inclusive

doing to being requires participants to experience a deep inner shift. In research amongst leaders,[22] I identified this shift as a "consequential transition,"[23, 24] which is a conscious, reflective struggle to make sense of what they have experienced. This struggle may result in them seeing themselves and others differently both in the space of the training programme and once they have returned to work. This shift is consequential because it matters to them and to those around them. Bringing about this shift requires a learning experience where participants are challenged at the cognitive and emotional and behavioural levels.

Working with leaders to create a consequential transition requires working with a range of teaching and learning tools. One of these is working with leaders' histories, encouraging them to gain an understanding of how their pasts have shaped their identities and their attitudes towards inclusion. Through exploring their personal stories, leaders are provided with a route to have different types of conversations with those around them. In encouraging storytelling around leaders' lives, we are able to have a broader conversation around identity and inclusion.

Consequential transitions are about changing your sense of self and your behaviour through gaining a deeper level of self-awareness. This is about creating a new understanding and, potentially, a new identity. An example of this shift is when white leaders recognise themselves as racialised as white and begin to think through the implications this has for them at work. This is an aspect of their leadership identity that they may not have considered before. However, this shift can be difficult if you are the only one in your team or organisation who is making it. Making inclusion stick over the long term may require a deep, immersive learning experience that encourages this shift from doing to being.

Being different is about making space to gain an understanding of the black leadership experience. This requires time to develop relationships, educate yourself and understand the impact of your biases. It also necessitates a shift from awareness to action, being prepared to call out behaviours that are not okay. Making the shift from doing inclusion to truly being inclusive necessitates deeper work on who you are as a leader.

KEY TAKEAWAYS

- There are six actions an individual can take to improve inclusion: educate themselves, understand white fragility, leverage their advantage, build relationships, recognise unacceptable behaviours and call them in or out.
- OPEN offers a way for white colleagues to work with race in the moment.
- Making the deeper shift from doing inclusion to being inclusive requires the experience of a "consequential transition."

QUESTIONS FOR REFLECTION

- What role can you play in making your workplace more inclusive?
- In which of the six areas can you do specific work?
- How could you use the OPEN framework?
- To what extent do you buy into the notion of the need to experience a "consequential transition?"

NOTES

1 Brienen, R. P. (2014). Types and Stereotypes: Zwarte Piet and His Early Modern Sources. In *Dutch Racism* (pp. 179–200). Amsterdam, New York: Brill.

2 Hermes, J. (2018). *Quoted in This Notorious Christmas Character Is Dividing a Country, National Geographic.* www.nationalgeographic.com/history/article/black-pete-christmas-zwarte-piet-dutch [Last accessed 28 July 2021].

3 Gergen, K. J. (1999). *An Invitation to Social Construction.* Thousand Oaks: Sage.

4 Stacey, R. (2012). *Tools and Techniques of Leadership and Management: Meeting the Challenge of Complexity.* Oxford, UK: Routledge.

5 Hirsch, A. (2018). *Brit(ish): On Race, Identity and Belonging.* London: Vintage.

6 Olusoga, D. (2016). *Black and British: A Forgotten History.* London: Pan Macmillan.

7 Gentleman, A. (2021). *The Windrush Betrayal: Exposing the Hostile Environment.* London, UK: Guardian Books.

8 Mc Queen, S. (2020). Small Axe (Anthology). *BBC*; Mc Queen, S. (2021). Small Axe (Anthology). *BBC*.

9 Kendi, I. X. (2019). *How to Be an Antiracist.* New York: One World.

10 Cooley. (2020). *Black Attorney Affinity Group Allyship + Anti-Racism Resource.* www.cooley.com/-/media/cooley/pdf/baag-allyship-and-antiracism-resource-kit.ashx [Last accessed 28 July 2021].

11 DiAngelo, R. (2019). *White Fragility.* United Kingdom: Penguin Books Ltd.

12 McIntosh, P. (2020). White Privilege and Male Privilege: A Personal Account of Coming to See Correspondences Through Work. *Privilege and Prejudice: Twenty Years with the Invisible Knapsack* 7; McIntosh, P. (1989, July–August). White Privilege: Unpacking the Invisible Knapsack. *Peace and Freedom* 10.

13 Aouragh, M. (2019). 'White Privilege' and Shortcuts to Anti-Racism. *Race & Class* 61(2), 3–26.

14 Frankenberg, R. (1993). *White Women, Race Matters: The Social Construction of Whiteness.* Minneapolis: University of Minnesota Press.

15 Kenny, B. (Host). (2021, February 2). Using Empathy and Curiosity to Overcome Differences. *Cold Call* (Episode 138). https://hbr.org/podcast/2021/02/using-empathy-and-curiosity-to-overcome-differences [Last accessed 28 July 2021].

16 Sue, D. et al. (2007). Racial Microaggressions in Everyday Life: Implications for Clinical Practice. *American Psychologist* 62(4), 271.

17 Sue, D. et al. (2007). Racial Microaggressions in Everyday Life: Implications for Clinical Practice. *American Psychologist* 62(4), 271.

18 Williams, M. T. (2020). *Managing Microaggressions: Addressing Everyday Racism in Therapeutic Spaces.* New York: Oxford University Press.

19 Sue, D. et al. (2007). Racial Microaggressions in Everyday Life: Implications for Clinical Practice. *American Psychologist* 62(4), 271.

20 Sue, D. W., Alsaidi, S., Awad, M. N., Glaeser, E., Calle, C. Z., & Mendez, N. (2019). Disarming Racial Microaggressions: Microintervention Strategies for Targets, White Allies, and Bystanders. *American Psychologist* 74(1), 128.

21 Banda, B. (2011). *Connecting Management Education with the Workplace* (Doctoral dissertation, DPhil thesis, University of Oxford, Oxford).

22 Banda, B. (2011). *Connecting Management Education with the Workplace* (Doctoral dissertation, DPhil thesis, University of Oxford, Oxford).

23 Beach, K. (1999). Chapter 4: Consequential Transitions: A Sociocultural Expedition Beyond Transfer in Education. *Review of Research in Education* 24(1), 101–139; Amer Educational Research Assn

24 Beach, K. (2003). Consequential Transitions: A Developmental View of Knowledge Propagation Through Social Organization. In T. Tumio-Grohn (Ed.), *Between School and Work, New Perspective on Transfer and Boundary-Crossing* (pp. 39–61). Amsterdam, London; Pergamon.

REFERENCES AND ADDITIONAL READING

Aouragh, M. (2019). 'White Privilege' and Shortcuts to Anti-Racism. *Race & Class* 61(2), 3–26.

Banda, B. (2011). *Connecting Management Education with the Workplace* (Doctoral dissertation, DPhil thesis, University of Oxford, Oxford).

Beach, K. (1999). Chapter 4: Consequential Transitions: A Sociocultural Expedition Beyond Transfer in Education. *Review of Research in Education* 24(1), 101–139. Amer Educational Research Assn

Beach, K. (2003). Consequential Transitions: A Developmental View of Knowledge Propagation Through Social Organization. In T. Tumio-Grohn, & Y. Engeström (Eds.), *Between School and Work, New Perspective on Transfer and Boundary-Crossing* (pp. 39–61). Amsterdam, London: Pergamon.

Blume, B. D., Ford, J. K., Baldwin, T. T., & Huang, J. L. (2010). Transfer of Training: A Meta-Analytic Review. *Journal of Management* 36(4), 1065–1105.

Brienen, R. P. (2014). Types and Stereotypes: Zwarte Piet and His Early Modern Sources. In P. Essed, & I. Hoving (Eds.), *Dutch Racism* (pp. 179–200). Amsterdam, New York: Rodopi.

Brown, J. (2019). *How to Be an Inclusive Leader: Your Role in Creating Cultures of Belonging Where Everyone Can Thrive*. Oakland, CA: Berrett-Koehler Publishers.

Burke, L. A., & Hutchins, H. M. (2008). A Study of Best Practices in Training Transfer and Proposed Model of Transfer. *Human Resource Development Quarterly* 19(2), 107–128.

Cooley. (2020). *Black Attorney Affinity Group Allyship + Anti-Racism Resource*. www.cooley.com/-/media/cooley/pdf/baag-allyship-and-antiracism-resource-kit.ashx [Last accessed 28 July 2021].

DiAngelo, R. (2019). *White Fragility*. United Kingdom: Penguin Books Ltd.

Frankenberg, R. (1993). *White Women, Race Matters: The Social Construction of Whiteness*. Minneapolis: University of Minnesota Press.

Gentleman, A. (2021). *The Windrush Betrayal: Exposing the Hostile Environment*. London, UK: Guardian Books.

Gergen, K. J. (1999). *An Invitation to Social Construction*. Thousand Oaks. Sage.

Hermes, J. (2018). *Quoted in This Notorious Christmas Character Is Dividing a Country, National Geographic*. www.nationalgeographic.com/history/article/black-pete-christmas-zwarte-piet-dutch [Last accessed 28 July 2021].

Hilhorst, S., & Hermes, J. (2016). 'We Have Given up so Much': Passion and Denial in the Dutch Zwarte Piet (Black Pete) Controversy. *European Journal of Cultural Studies* 19(3), 218–233.

Hirsch, A. (2018). *Brit(ish): On Race, Identity and Belonging*. London: Vintage.

Kendall, F. (2012). *Understanding White Privilege: Creating Pathways to Authentic Relationships Across Race*. United Kingdom: Routledge.

Kendi, I. X. (2019). *How to Be an Antiracist*. New York: One World.

Kenny, B. (Host). (2021, February 2). Using Empathy and Curiosity to Overcome Differences. *Cold Call* (Episode 138). https://hbr.org/podcast/2021/02/using-empathy-and-curiosity-to-overcome-differences [Last accessed 28 July 2021].

Lievens, F., Harrison, S., Mussel, P., & Litman, J. (2021). Killing the Cat? A Review of Curiosity at Work. *Academy of Management Annals* 16(1).

McIntosh, P. (1989, July–August). White Privilege: Unpacking the Invisible Knapsack. *Peace and Freedom* 10.

McIntosh, P. (2020). White Privilege and Male Privilege: A Personal Account of Coming to see Correspondences through Work. *Privilege and Prejudice: Twenty Years with the Invisible Knapsack* 7.

Mc Queen, S. (2020). Small Axe (Anthology). *BBC*.

Mc Queen, S. (2021). Small Axe (Anthology). *BBC*.

Olusoga, D. (2016). *Black and British: A Forgotten History*. London: Pan Macmillan.

Rodenberg, J., & Wagenaar, P. (2016). Essentializing 'Black Pete': Competing Narratives Surrounding the Sinterklaas Tradition in the Netherlands. *International Journal of Heritage Studies* 22(9), 716–728.

Shaw, P. (2003). *Changing Conversations in Organizations: A Complexity Approach to Change*. London: Routledge.

Stacey, R. (2012). *Tools and Techniques of Leadership and Management: Meeting the Challenge of Complexity*. Oxford: Routledge.

Sue, D. et al. (2007). Racial Microaggressions in Everyday Life: Implications for Clinical Practice. *American Psychologist* 62(4), 271.

Sue, D. W., Alsaidi, S., Awad, M. N., Glaeser, E., Calle, C. Z., & Mendez, N. (2019). Disarming Racial Microaggressions: Microintervention Strategies for Targets, White Allies, and Bystanders. *American Psychologist* 74(1), 128.

Williams, M. T. (2020). *Managing Microaggressions: Addressing Everyday Racism in Therapeutic Spaces*. New York: Oxford University Press.

9

"WE ALL WANT EQUITY – DON'T WE?"

This chapter

- *outlines three areas where organisations can do further work to improve inclusion and diversity,*
- *examines the research on what works in improving inclusion in organisations and*
- *proposes an organisational OPEN framework for continuous action.*

You have to hire a chief diversity officer. . . . They have to be high enough in the company, and they need to be the advocate for the CEO and the board to ensure that diversity and inclusion are being executed successfully throughout the company.

> Michael Sherman, Chief Strategy and
> Transformation Officer, BT

Too often, we get caught up in, "We want the best person for the job." No one's saying we don't want the best person for the job. What we're saying is we want to ensure that we have an inclusive workforce with the best people to get the job done. Don't fall into that trap and be saying, "We hired one less white person, so we're not as good as would have been because we had to hire an unqualified black person." That's just false. It's just untrue. There are enough qualified people to be hired.

> Anon, Senior Executive, IT

I think it involves black and white people. I don't think it is right to just target the black people. The same way you need to talk to both men and women about gender, you need to talk to both black and white people to come to a common understanding about race.

Lorna Matty, People Development Manager, Toyota

People aren't actively excluding people, not consciously necessarily, but the behaviours and what they expect of people and by implication, they're excluding people. This exclusion often occurs by accident, which is where some form of training, or informal reverse mentoring can be useful.

Paul Cleal, OBE, Former Partner, PwC

They have some type of quota for women in executive positions . . . but they're not going to put a quota on how many Black executives they have in those positions. I do know why they're scared because the CEO told me: "What we do for black people, we've got to do for everybody."

Anon, Senior Executive, Manufacturing

As discussed in Chapter 8, an organisation is not a single "thing" but is composed of many individuals.[1] How an organisation develops and changes depends not only on the choices of its leaders but also on the microinteractions between individuals. It is here that behaviours in the organisation are changed or sustained. Consequently, the suggestions offered to individuals in Chapter 8 to improve understanding and inclusion are equally relevant for organisations.

Organisations spend millions of pounds each year in their quest to be more diverse, equitable and inclusive places to work. According to the Chartered Institute of Personnel and Development (CIPD),[2] becoming more diverse is about recognising difference, acknowledging the benefit of having a range of perspectives in decision-making and the workforce is representative of the organisation's customers and community. This means having people from a range of racial, ethnic, cultural and socioeconomic backgrounds and of different genders and sexual orientations and those with disabilities. The leaders I spoke with stressed that diversity goes beyond any visible difference to include a range of talents, skills and opinions. By "equitable," they meant spaces where there were equal opportunities, where individuals from all backgrounds are given the resources to achieve, requiring specific support for different groups to allow them to reach their full potential. Inclusion is understood as ensuring that the work environment is a space where everyone feels valued. It is about how it feels to work in the organisation. Establishing an environment of inclusion requires understanding, collaboration and respect from all sides.

The rationale for accelerating inclusion is clear. The business case for creating more inclusive organisations was discussed in Chapter 1. More important is the moral case. Having a work environment where all individuals are treated equally and with dignity has to be the right thing to do in the 21st-century workplace. However, there is a gap between organisations' good intentions and the outcomes, especially as it relates to the black leaders of British organisations interviewed for this book. This gap is underlined by the McGregor-Smith report,[3] which said of BAME employees, "There is discrimination and bias at every stage of an individual's career, and even before it begins. From networks to recruitment and then in the workforce, it is there." This means that organisations need to consider what approaches they are using to hire black candidates, where they are recruiting and what wording is used. Efforts also need to be made to monitor the progress of black leaders once they enter organisations to ensure they fulfil their potential.

Incentives are being put in place to encourage positive change. In 2020, many top American corporations announced that they would link executive pay to progress in diversity.[4] Organisations including McDonald's, Starbucks and American Express have decided to tie diversity goals to executive compensation. Fifteen per cent of executive bonuses at McDonald's are tied to meeting targets including those for D&I. It has also begun disclosing data on the racial make-up of its workforce. This strong focus is needed because progress towards specific goals had not been sufficiently tracked over time, and there were not many board questions on diversity. There was concern that unless board compensation is tied to diversity outcomes, then things would not change.

Based on the interviews and research, I have identified three areas where organisations can improve their diversity, equity and inclusion. These form the rooms of the DEI House (Figure 9.1).

Figure 9.1 The DEI House

BEST PRACTICE: UNDERSTAND WHAT DOES WORK

There are no easy solutions in the quest for greater black representation in senior roles or improving inclusion more broadly in the workplace. However, not all initiatives are assessed. In their 2016 report for the Policy Exchange, Saggar[5] and colleagues found that although there is widespread support for greater diversity, there is surprisingly little awareness about the most effective levers to achieve it. They identified that diversity professionals are not well connected to academic or research practitioner evidence. As a result, best practices are slow to be shared, and there is a need to consolidate the evidence base. Dobbin and Kalev[6] analysed three decades of data from over 800 US firms and interviewed hundreds of line managers and executives at length to understand what works. In relation to black men and women, their research found the following:

- *Training.* Voluntary diversity training led to a 13.3 per cent increase in black men. Mandatory training led to a 6 to 9 per cent drop across all minorities. A fundamental problem is that mandatory training is often positioned as remedial, and therefore managers disengage.
- *Mentoring.* This was associated with an 18 per cent increase in black women. However, there is a risk of backlash if sponsorship is seen as part of an affirmative action initiative

- *D&I specialists.* Having diversity managers in place contributed to a 17 per cent increase in black men and an 11.1 per cent increase in black women. When a diversity task force was set up, that figure increased to 8.7 per cent for women and 22.7 per cent for men. The risk here is that those advocating diversity can face criticism from colleagues.
- *Self-managed teams.* When black men and women worked side by side with white colleagues as equals, there was an increase of 3.4 per cent for men and 3.9 per cent for women.
- *Hiring tests.* There was evidence that results were ignored when white men failed. Written tests resulted in a decrease of 10 per cent of black men and 9 per cent of black women in managerial jobs.
- *Performance ratings.* Evidence that women and minorities are graded lower in ratings. No effect on the number of minority managers.

In a similar vein, a comprehensive review of over 40 years of research on diversity training in the US by Bezrukova and colleagues[7] showed that diversity training can produce long-term cognitive learning. They suggested that this "stickiness" may be because, after training, there are cues in the workplace or elsewhere that could reinforce the learning. The review identified three main factors that contribute to effective training. First, diversity training has been most useful when training is part of other broader organisational initiatives. Second, training is more effective when it takes place over multiple sessions. Third, the training needs to focus on both awareness and skills.

Similar data for the UK is not available.

This data does not mean that other forms of inclusive initiatives and practices are ineffective, but rather that the relevant evidence may not have been collected. However, the aforementioned data offers specific areas where organisations can focus and measure their efforts.

USE BEST PRACTICES IN RECRUITMENT, RETENTION AND PROMOTION

Recruitment, retention and promotion are areas where bias can be a problem. One leader informed me how she sat on an interview panel with two white men and a white woman. They had clear objective criteria. One of the candidates was a white male with a "southern" UK accent. The second was a black male who had a Nigerian accent. She noticed how much more at ease her white panel members were with the white male. They laughed with him at his slight clumsiness; they engaged in small talk about his university experiences; they exchanged experiences on the education of their school-aged children. There was no such introductory conversation with the Nigerian male. The leader told me how she listened carefully to what the Nigerian said, and his answers scored higher against all the criteria. Yet, the white colleagues claimed they found him hard to understand. There is no substitute for bias awareness on the part of the decision-makers. Those same decision-makers need to be open to understanding and talking about bias. Herein lies the challenge. When the white applicant was selected in the previous example, the black leader found that her fellow panellists did not want to talk about bias. You can have the best procedures in place, but they are only as good as those following them. Hence changes in attitudes to recruitment and promotion need to be part of broader culture change initiatives.

In her report, McGregor-Smith[8] offers five clear recommendations for increasing diversity at the recruitment stage:

- Rejecting non-diverse shortlists
- Challenging educational selection
- Drafting job specifications in a more inclusive way
- Introducing diversity to interview panels
- Creating work experience opportunities for everyone, not just the chosen few

Additional detailed recruitment best practice is available from the CIPD (www.cipd.co.uk/).[9]

With respect to retention, organisations should focus on creating a climate where they feel comfortable. Recommendations include the following:

- Organisations should promote a climate where the activities listed in Chapter 8 become accepted and normalised.
- Promote the activities that have been proven to work in promoting inclusion and diversity.

- Do not just sign the Race at Work Charter – collect and publish your data. Live it!
- Allow "black only spaces." Establish an Employee Resource Group and give it the freedom to agree on purpose and activities.
- Senior leadership needs to be seen to be actively working to diminish bias in performance and promotion.
- Senior leaders should be seen to reject and reprimand unacceptable behaviours.
- Senior leaders need to create a climate where black leaders can be more authentic and feel as supported as their white colleagues.
- Senior leaders need to feel comfortable talking about race.

When it comes to the promotion of black employees, Saggar and colleagues[10] noted their frustration with the limited extent to which data are available on progression at the top of companies. They point to the following five suggestions for improving promotion which also emerged in the research for this book:

Voluntary targets. Many of the leaders interviewed for this book are against compulsory targets for black leaders. Two leaders stated that lessons could be learnt from the efforts to increase the numbers of women at senior levels. There was concern that targets should be for black not BAME leaders so that black leaders could be promoted and counted.

The Rooney Rule. Ensuring that a black candidate is put forward for each senior-level role. One of the leaders interviewed complained that his senior leadership team did not understand the concept. They felt it was about finding any black candidate, and he had to constantly argue that this was always about finding a suitably qualified candidate.

Batch appointments. Where possible, build a process of group recruitment at senior levels to illuminate where biases are present. It also makes it harder for employers to defend biased outcomes.

Learn from the success of the Davies Review.[11] The 2011 Davies Review presented recommendations to address the gender imbalance on the boards of FTSE 350 companies. It proposed setting targets and disclosing the number of women on boards. Since its publication, the percentage of women serving on FTSE 360 boards increased from 9 per cent in 2011 to 34 per cent in 2021. As well as proposing goals for the number of women, one of its suggestions was that success breeds success when it comes to numbers. Men see more women on boards and therefore buy into the idea. The same is needed for black faces.

Find ways of tapping into the pipeline. Have processes that ensure that everyone who could be promoted puts themselves forward. Large companies can use detailed metrics of staff performance to select potential candidates for promotion without them being known to company leaders.

DO NOT IGNORE THE POWER OF BIAS IN THE ORGANISATION

Half of the black leaders spoke of the importance of the challenges of bias. We all have biases – research suggests as many as 200 of them – that provide us with shortcuts in decision-making. Our unconscious biases cause us to make judgements based on our previous experiences, thought patterns and assumptions. Neuroscientists tell us that the areas of our brain that form certain biases can be seen from early childhood. Indeed, in our early lives, we have a predisposition to like the kinds of people surrounding us.[12] As we develop, our attitudes are then shaped by the cultural values that we are exposed to and the education we receive. Our unconscious brain works through vast amounts of information as it seeks out patterns. Our brain then expects to see certain things together – for example, female midwives or white middle-aged senior leaders in certain organisations. The result is that other patterns appear less normal. There is evidence that these biases affect our behaviour.[13] Bias awareness helps us to notice these patterns so that we can try to avoid stereotyping or prejudicial behaviour. This awareness can help us make good decisions about our colleagues and their contributions, particularly when those colleagues are different from us. The inclination to employ, promote and just be around people like us is a tendency most of us have to fight against. "He is not the right fit" is a common euphemism for "he is black."

Is training the answer? A study by the Equalities and Human Rights Commission[14] suggests a mixed picture around the effectiveness of unconscious bias training and identified the need for further studies in the area. The authors noted that there is evidence such training can raise awareness and limit individuals' use of implicit bias. However, they claim that the evidence for its ability effectively to change behaviour is limited. The report's authors are wary of the potential for unconscious bias training to backfire if they are exposed to information that suggests stereotypes and biases are unchangeable. There has been a lot of debate around the use of unconscious bias training, with the UK Civil Service phasing it out because of a lack of evidence that it promotes change.[15] However, others argue that such training can yield benefits;[16] the problem with unconscious bias training is how such training is delivered.[17]

Indeed, problems can arise when unconscious bias training is obligatory and is done as a stand-alone initiative over the short term. Unconscious bias training needs to be part of a broader initiative to change the behaviours and ultimately the organisation's culture. This notion resonates with my experience of working with bias as part of broader inclusive leadership development initiatives. In these cases, leaders have time to consider how these biases might play out in their ability to include others in the workplace and work through pragmatic ways to bring about lasting personal change.

UNDERSTAND THE "BLACK TAX"

A third of those in this study raised the issue of the black tax as the emotional and physical price black leaders pay for being part of an under-represented group. Being the only black person in the department, function, division or organisation can take a lot of energy. The expectation that you should then take on the extra tasks of leading an inclusion task force or being the "black ambassador" for the organisation becomes exhausting. It's even more depleting when you are also, then, invited to have courageous conversations with your well-meaning white colleagues. Throughout this, black leaders are still expected to complete their work to a higher standard than many of their white colleagues. It is very demoralising when this effort is not credited in an annual performance review.

Black leaders talked about the energy required to take on extra work regarding EDI. One spoke of how frustrating it was to put in all of this extra work only to find that white colleagues still did not "get it." Another described feeling like being a celebrity without any of the positive trappings of fame. Black leaders want this work to be recognised as part of the performance review process. One leader talked about organisations where this was beginning to happen.

White leaders can also get involved in this kind of work, volunteering to help. Black leaders complained that there was often a lot of administrative work involved, which their white colleagues could share.

Do not assume a quid pro quo

A second tax is the assumption that because you have done everything the black leaders in this study asked, they will open up and share details of their everyday experiences with you. They might not. There is a lot of evidence in this book that black people are wary of opening up because they have previously experienced negative consequences. One leader recalled sharing her views on what being black in Britain was like in what she felt was the safe space of a leadership programme. Her experiences were invalidated, so she decided never to share again. She had been misunderstood and labelled. In addition, talking about experiences can feel like revisiting the trauma or scratching an open wound. It's not something that some black people want to return to again and again. So, if your black colleague does not want to talk, then leave them alone. Respect the idea that you may never truly understand the experience of that particular black person.

There was also the belief among some respondents that there was not always a case for black people to tell their stories to bring about change. One leader argued,

> You do not approach a domestic violence victim and say, "I need you to tell me about your experience so that I can understand that violence against women is wrong." You just *know* it's wrong. Racism is like that – you know it's wrong. You don't need to hear my lived experience to understand that.

Allow me to bring more of myself to work

"Thank goodness she has settled in!" This is the comment I often hear when a newcomer to the organisation no longer asks questions about why things are done in a certain way. I have observed how individuals are brought into organisations for diversity and then managed for sameness. Organisations use shame as a process to ensure that individuals fit in and abide by the existing social norms.[18] Individuals are blamed and shamed for infringing social norms. The correct behaviour is encouraged, and wrong behaviour is rooted out through shaming the perpetrators. So, we copy and shame each other in equal measure. When black leaders join an organisation, they may exhibit behaviours that are acceptable in their own social settings but are made to feel that they need to leave them behind and conform completely to progress. This process of adopting the profile and the behaviours of the Model Black means that a lot of the difference is left at home. Black leaders want white leaders to give them the space to bring more of themselves to work. "They don't know black people, and therefore if you're a little bit loud, you're a bit too informal, as sometimes we are, they take that as some kind of handicap."

Hence, the third tax is the pressure of leaving a large part of themselves at home. Black leaders want you to treat them "in the same way as they treat white people." They also want their differences to be encouraged and accepted.

And please see – and respond to – my colour!

It was against the backdrop of the Black Lives Matter movement in 2020 that one of the black leaders interviewed for this book – the only senior person of colour in her organisation – plucked up the courage to write a short post expressing her response to the death of George Floyd. Consequently, a number of her colleagues called her to explain that they never saw her as a black person – they simply saw her for who she is. They continued to have the impression that seeing colour somehow means that you harbour prejudices. She wanted to reply, "When you say that, it means you don't see my difference, and the value that I bring because I'm different. That's the issue with that, and if you don't see colour, that means you're never going to recognise that there needs to be more people like me in this room."

Not seeing black people means lots of negative things to black leaders. It means that you do not need to accept that race might be an issue, that you do not have to enter into uncomfortable conversations around race. Black leaders *want* their colleagues to see colour. They want colleagues to understand that they bring something different, that they may have had different experiences which influence their contributions. My wonderful Dutch friend Carry acted the way she did because she did not see colour.

This fourth tax is therefore the experience of having your difference ignored.

The importance of seeing colour at more than a superficial level was universal amongst the black leaders in this study. Some cautioned against racial window dressing. The act of appointing black people to certain positions and then making no changes to the culture of the organisation was a particular bugbear: "Do not make out whilst you are still terrorising existing staff members that you're spending money and giving this illusion that you are doing something about inclusion."

BE OPEN AS AN ORGANISATION

I propose an adaptation of the OPEN framework described in Chapter 8 as a framework for organisations to consider the extent to which they are implementing inclusive practices in relation to their black employees:

Observe	• How aware are we of the black experience in our organisation? • What does our data tell us about the recruitment, promotion and retention of black workers?
Perspective	• What best practices are we employing to enhance diversity equity and inclusion? • How are our leaders reviewed and rewarded against our best practice initiatives?
Engage	• How can we engage with black leaders to allow them to be open about their experience? • How can we ensure that we have the best processes to understand how our actions are contributing to the black leadership experience?
Next	• Who needs to be involved in the vision and goal setting for the future? • What trusted third party can support us on our journey?

KEY TAKEAWAYS

- The DEI House consists of three "rooms" where organisations can focus on improving their diversity, equity and inclusion.
- Organisations must understand the evidence base for diversity, equity and inclusion initiatives and use it to inform future activities.
- Understanding and minimising bias in recruitment, retention and promotion is an important step to improving inclusion.
- The "black taxes" should be appreciated and minimised.
- The OPEN framework provides a guide for organisational considerations.

QUESTIONS FOR REFLECTION

- How well is your organisation communicating its DEI strategy? How can you check for understanding?
- To what extent are your senior leaders "walking the talk" in relation to inclusion strategy?
- What Diversity, Equity and Inclusion initiatives do you have in place, and how do you measure their impact?
- To what extent is your organisation staying OPEN?

NOTES

1 Stacey, R. D. (2011). *Strategic Management and Organisational Dynamics*. Harlow: Pearson.
2 CIPD. (2021). Inclusion and Diversity in the Workplace. *Factsheet*. www.cipd.co.uk/knowledge/fundamentals/relations/diversity/factsheet#gref [Last accessed 29 July 2021].
3 McGregor-Smith, R. (2017). *Race in the Workplace: The McGregor-Smith Review, UK Government*. https://assets.publishing.service.gov.uk/government/uploads/system/uploads/attachment_data/file/594336/race-in-workplace-mcgregor-smith-review.pdf [Last accessed 11 April 2021].
4 Glazer, E., & Francis, T (2021, June 2). CEO Pay Increasingly Tied to Diversity Goals. *Wall Street Journal*. www.wsj.com/articles/ceos-pledged-to-increase-diversity-now-boards-are-holding-them-to-it-11622626380

[Last accessed November 2021]; McDonald's Corp. (2021). *Diversity, Equity and Inclusion.* https://corporate.mcdonalds.com/corpmcd/our-purpose-and-impact/jobs-inclusion-and-empowerment/diversity-and-inclusion.html [Last accessed November 2021]; Smith, A. (2021, July 12). *More Companies Use DE&I as Executive Compensation Metric.* www.shrm.org/resourcesand-tools/legal-and-compliance/employment-law/pages/dei-as-executive-compensation-metric.aspx [Last accessed November 2021].

5 Saggar, S., Norrie, R., Bannister, M., & Goodhart, D. (2016). Bittersweet Success? Glass Ceilings for Britain's Ethnic Minorities at the Top of Business and the Professions. *Policy Exchange.* https://policyexchange.org.uk/wp-content/uploads/2016/11/Bittersweet-Success-Glass-Ceiling-FINAL-DRAFT.pdf.

6 Dobbin, F., & Kalev, A. (2016). Why Diversity Programs Fail. *Harvard Business Review* 94(7), 14.

7 Bezrukova, K., Spell, C. S., Perry, J. L., & Jehn, K. A. (2016). A Meta-Analytical Integration of Over 40 Years of Research on Diversity Training Evaluation. *Psychological Bulletin* 142(11), 1227.

8 McGregor-Smith, R. (2017). *Race in the Workplace: The McGregor-Smith Review, UK Government.* https://assets.publishing.service.gov.uk/government/uploads/system/uploads/attachment_data/file/594336/race-in-workplace-mcgregor-smith-review.pdf [Last accessed 11 April 2021].

9 CIPD. (2021). Inclusion and Diversity in the Workplace. *Factsheet.* www.cipd.co.uk/knowledge/fundamentals/relations/diversity/factsheet#gref [Last accessed 29 July 2021].

10 Saggar, S., Norrie, R., Bannister, M., & Goodhart, D. (2016). Bittersweet Success? Glass Ceilings for Britain's Ethnic Minorities at the Top of Business and the Professions. *Policy Exchange.* https://policyexchange.org.uk/wp-content/uploads/2016/11/Bittersweet-Success-Glass-Ceiling-FINAL-DRAFT.pdf.

11 Lord Davies of Abersoch et al. (2011). *Women on Boards.* London: Department of Business Innovation and Skills.

12 Kinzler, K. D., Dupoux, E., & Spelke, E. S. (2007). The Native Language of Social Cognition. *Proceedings of the National Academy of Sciences* 104(30), 12577–12580.

13 Banaji, M. R., & Greenwald, A. G. (2016). *Blindspot: Hidden Biases of Good People.* New York: Bantam Books; Banaji, M. R., Bhaskar, R., & Brownstein, M. (2015). When Bias Is Implicit, How Might We Think about Repairing Harm? *Current Opinion in Psychology* 6, 183–188.

14 Atewologun, D., Cornish, T., & Tresh, F. (2018). Unconscious Bias Training: An Assessment of the Evidence for Effectiveness. *Equality and Human Rights Commission Research Report Series.* Equality and Human Rights Commission.

15 GOV.UK. (2020). *Written Ministerial Statement on Unconscious Bias Training: WMS laid in the House of Commons on Tuesday 15th December 2020.* www.gov.uk/government/news/written-ministerial-statement-on-unconscious-bias-training [Last accessed 20 July 2021].

16 Girod, S., Fassiotto, M., Grewal, D., Ku, M. C., Sriram, N., Nosek, B. A., & Valantine, H. (2016). Reducing Implicit Gender Leadership Bias in Academic Medicine with an Educational Intervention. *Academic Medicine* 91(8), 1143–1150.

17 Emerson, J. (2017, April). Don't Give Up on Unconscious Bias Training – Make It Better. *Harvard Business Review* 28.

18 Stacey, R. D. (2011). *Strategic Management and Organisational Dynamics.* Harlow: Pearson.

REFERENCES AND ADDITIONAL READING

Atewologun, D., Cornish, T., & Tresh, F. (2018). Unconscious Bias Training: An Assessment of the Evidence for Effectiveness. Equality and Human Rights Commission Research Report Series. Equality and Human Rights Commission.

Banaji, M. R., Bhaskar, R., & Brownstein, M. (2015). When Bias Is Implicit, How Might We Think about Repairing Harm? *Current Opinion in Psychology 6*, 183–188.

Banaji, M. R., & Greenwald, A. G. (2016). *Blindspot: Hidden Biases of Good People.* New York: Bantam Books.

Bezrukova, K., Spell, C. S., Perry, J. L., & Jehn, K. A. (2016). A Meta-Analytical Integration of Over 40 Years of Research on Diversity Training Evaluation. *Psychological Bulletin* 142(11), 1227.

Business in the Community. *Race at Work Charter.* www.bitc.org.uk/post_tag/race-at-work-charter/ [Last accessed 20 July 2021].

CIPD. (2021). Inclusion and Diversity in the Workplace. *Factsheet.* www.cipd.co.uk/knowledge/fundamentals/relations/diversity/factsheet#gref [Last accessed 29 July 2021].

Dobbin, F., & Kalev, A. (2016). Why Diversity Programs Fail. *Harvard Business Review* 94(7), 14.

Emerson, J. (2017, April). Don't Give Up on Unconscious Bias Training – Make It Better. *Harvard Business Review* 28.

Girod, S., Fassiotto, M., Grewal, D., Ku, M. C., Sriram, N., Nosek, B. A., & Valantine, H. (2016). Reducing Implicit Gender Leadership Bias in Academic Medicine with an Educational Intervention. *Academic Medicine* 91(8), 1143–1150.

Glazer, E., & Francis, T (2021, June 2). CEO Pay Increasingly Tied to Diversity Goals. *Wall Street Journal.* www.wsj.com/articles/ceos-pledged-to-increase-diversity-now-boards-are-holding-them-to-it-11622626380 [Last accessed November 2021].

GOV.UK. (2020). *Written Ministerial Statement on Unconscious Bias Training: WMS Laid in the House of Commons on Tuesday 15th December 2020.* www.gov.uk/government/news/written-ministerial-statement-on-unconscious-bias-training [Last accessed 20 July 2021].

Harts, M. (2019). *The Memo: What Women of Color Need to Know to Secure a Seat at the Table.* New York: Hachette.

Kalev, A., Dobbin, F., & Kelly, E. (2006). Best Practices or Best Guesses? Assessing the Efficacy of Corporate Affirmative Action and Diversity Policies. *American Sociological Review* 71(4), 589–617.

Kinzler, K. D., Dupoux, E., & Spelke, E. S. (2007). The Native Language of Social Cognition. *Proceedings of the National Academy of Sciences* 104(30), 12577–12580.

Lord Davies of Abersoch et al. (2011). *Women on Boards.* London: Department of Business Innovation and Skills.

McDonald's Corp. (2021). *Diversity, Equity and Inclusion.* https://corporate.mcdonalds.com/corpmcd/our-purpose-and-impact/jobs-inclusion-and-empowerment/diversity-and-inclusion.html [Last accessed November 2021].

McGregor-Smith, R. (2017). *Race in the Workplace: The McGregor-Smith Review, UK Government.* https://assets.publishing.service.gov.uk/government/uploads/system/uploads/attachment_data/file/594336/race-in-workplace-mcgregor-smith-review.pdf [Last accessed 11 April 2021].

Mor Barak, M. E. (2016). *Managing Diversity: Toward a Globally Inclusive Workplace.* United Kingdom: SAGE Publications.

Oluo, I. (2019). *So You Want to Talk about Race?* UK: Hachette.

Pronin, E., Lin, D. Y., & Ross, L. (2002). The Bias Blind Spot: Perceptions of Bias in Self versus Others. *Personality and Social Psychology Bulletin* 28(3), 369–381.

Saggar, S., Norrie, R., Bannister, M., & Goodhart, D. (2016). Bittersweet Success? Glass Ceilings for Britain's Ethnic Minorities at the Top of Business and the Professions. *Policy Exchange.* https://policyexchange.org.uk/wp-content/uploads/2016/11/Bittersweet-Success-Glass-Ceiling-FINAL-DRAFT.pdf.

Smith, A (2021, July 12). *More Companies Use DE&I as Executive Compensation Metric.* www.shrm.org/resourcesandtools/legal-and-compliance/employment-law/pages/dei-as-executive-compensation-metric.aspx [Last accessed November 2021].

Stacey, R. D. (2011). *Strategic Management and Organisational Dynamics.* Harlow: Pearson.

10

BEYOND THE MODEL BLACK?

This chapter

- *considers whether the new younger generation of black leaders need to be the Model Black to be successful,*
- *investigates the experiences of young black professionals in today's workplaces,*
- *explores alternatives to the Model Black trope and*
- *discusses the future of the Model Black.*

> In addition to the job you already have, you still need to also come up with this drama performance piece every single day.
>
> Anon Young Professional, Professional Services

> That's another insecurity that I find a lot of black people might have, holding themselves to an impossible standard, not giving themselves room to learn or to grow or to make mistakes, and that causes a tentativeness and a self-protection instinct that doesn't allow you to take risks, put your hand up for stuff.
>
> Anon Young Professional, Consultancy

> You definitely have to take the bass out of your voice.
>
> Anon Young Professional, Consultancy

> They can't make eye contact with you. You know when people just aren't comfortable around you. They don't sit right. Their voice is a bit higher than it otherwise is. They're not relaxed. They don't want to have a conversation with you, and they

DOI: 10.4324/9781003200482-15

don't want to be caught one-on-one with you. They're a bit awkward and don't really know what to say, and it's not like social awkwardness because they're perfectly fine with everyone else except me.

Anon Young Professional, Manufacturing

I want you to see the blackness, but I don't want you to see only the blackness. I want you to see me.

Anon Young Professional, Manufacturing

COMING OUT AS BLACK

In writing this book, I have outed myself as black.

I am borrowing this self-disclosure term which is associated with sexual orientation and gender identity. In my case, it is about talking about a part of myself that has always been visible but not spoken of in public and not spoken about in such candid terms. I have been accompanied in this process by the interviewees who took part in my research. Some have been named, some chose not to be named and others I chose not to name.

When I started the research for this book, the intention was to identify how black leaders successfully navigate their work environments. I wanted to share their strategies and advice. The hope was that in so doing, I could move the needle even a tiny amount towards making workplaces more inclusive spaces for current and future black workers. I also hoped that the findings might resonate with other under-represented groups in the workplace. As black leaders spoke candidly about their experiences, what emerged from the research was that the successful black leaders had much in common when they navigated race at work. The new Model Black trope emerged as encompassing many of the behaviours of the black leaders I spoke with. This was an unexpected finding.

The Model Black constitutes the *de facto* strategy for the majority of successful black leaders in this study. However, it is not my intention to propose this as the *recommended* strategy. It is the tried and tested strategy that black leaders employ to succeed at work. All the leaders exhibited aspects of the profile discussed in Chapter 4 and practiced some or all of the behaviours of squaring, softening and self-silencing to different extents.

Of note were the leaders who bucked the trend in relation to self-silencing. These were most likely to be working in non-corporate environments and also more likely to have achieved very senior positions. For example, Patricia Miller, OBE, chief executive at Dorset County Hospital Foundation Trust, told me that she has always spoken out about racism when she has experienced it. She may not have got the response that she wanted, but this had never stopped her. This was also the case for Grace Ononigu, CBE, director at the Crown Prosecution Service.

MILLENNIALS: A DIFFERENT WORKPLACE EXPERIENCE?

This book has intentionally focussed on successful black leaders working primarily in private sector organisations with a small number from the public sector. What this means is that they are necessarily of a certain age. Could it be that the next generation views things differently? Could it be that those currently in their 20s are having very different experiences in the workplace? There is often an optimism and energy for change which young people often experience early in their careers. However, I wanted to speak to a number of young black professionals to get a sense of how they are experiencing corporate life. Do the ideas of the Model Black resonate with them?

There are many generational stereotypes associated with millennials in the workplace: impatient, entitled and self-absorbed and wanting to find value and balance in their lives.[1]

However, the evidence suggests that the differences between generations with regards to attitudes to work may not be as large as we expect. A review of published and unpublished studies by Constanza[2] and colleagues showed on three work-related criteria – job satisfaction, organisational commitment and intent to turn over – that there were no meaningful differences across the generations. An IBM multigenerational study[3] of 1,784 employees from companies across 12 countries and six industries found the same approximate percentage of millennials want to make a positive impact on their organisations, help solve environmental challenges, work with a diverse group of people and do work that they enjoy as Gen Xers and Baby Boomers do.

With regard to issues of race, a generational divide was evident amongst white Americans in relation to the Black Lives Matter movement, with more millennials feeling that more needed to be done for black people than their parents and grandparents had done.[4] In the UK, there was evidence of large numbers of young people at the many Black Lives Matter demonstrations. However, it is hard to know whether this is the optimism and idealism of youth or whether there is something more significant happening amongst young people.

I spoke to six young professionals to gain their views on their experiences of race at work, and the following themes emerged.

The Model Black is still alive and kicking!

All of the young professionals' could identify with the nine success charateristics of black leaders discussed in Chapter 4. Furthermore, their behaviour resonated with the profile of the Model Black. Squaring, in particular, was identified as necessary to fit into white middle-class spaces. As with the older leaders, the extent to which this was required depended on their background. One young man expressed great delight at the ski trip being called off due to Covid-19! Or, as another young man put it, "You don't come from the same background. You don't have the same cultural cues. You don't speak the same way as people. You find out even the way you show respect to people is a bit different. For example, me growing up in a multi-ethnic environment and that kind of stuff, when you see someone in the corridor, it's as small as you give him a 'bro nod' as if you're saying, 'Are you all right?' kind of thing. That's a foreign concept in a place like this." The professionals grasped very early the onus was 100 per cent on them to adapt and fit in.

In relation to self-silencing, these young professionals said they were more likely to leave an organisation than "suck it up" if the culture was not right. They were very intolerant of overt racism yet also accepted that they would experience regular microaggressions. They were very aware of the structural reasons that would get in the way of their progression, such as the types of individuals who reached senior levels and the way appointments are made within their organisations. Their response was to work harder and keep their focus.

Softening was evident as I spoke to the men, where I was again struck by expressions of their warmth and sensitivity: "I was having a conversation with one of the senior managers, and I definitely watch every single aspect of him when I respond to something or when I say something, I was like, 'What did he think about that?'"

Greater comfort with talking about race at work – but challenges remain

The younger professionals had entered workplaces where, in many cases, black networks already existed. The major shift came for them in the wake of the death of George Floyd. One young professional told me how this event led to a shift in the way the network was perceived and the activities they were asked to get involved in. As a relatively new joiner, he valued the network as a social group where black workers could support each other. Post-Floyd, however, the group was forced to become more outward-facing, there to educate white colleagues and advocate on behalf of all blacks within the organisation. The group was asked to put forward a list of initiatives and changes that the organisation should get involved in. They were asked to run sessions with white colleagues to teach them how to talk about race. It had a positive impact. However, this proved exhausting – an unpaid element of the black tax.

One of the young female professionals, Tammy, told me how a white acquaintance had contacted her over the weekend about players "taking the knee" at the football European Football Championships. He wanted her to point him to some helpful resources. It demanded both emotional energy and time from Tammy to seek these things on a Saturday afternoon. However, she made an effort and sent him an email. She received no response. She has since seen the acquaintance twice at group events, and he had never referred to his request or her reply.

"As a white man, my colleague had the luxury of being able to dip into issues of race and politics on a Saturday afternoon and then forget about it." For Tammy, it was represented emotional labour that disturbed her relaxing weekend.

Companies are trying harder – but there is still a lot of subtle unpleasantness

Nicholas told me how he had been selected by three leading professional services companies. He had taken his time to consider where he would perform best and which organisation would offer the best development and promotion prospects. Equally important for him was the culture, specifically how he would fit in as a young black man. A key factor in his decision was the work the organisation was doing around inclusion. The organisation he chose is a signatory to the UK Business in the Community Race at Work Charter,[5] and it has a meaningful strategy that connects inclusion to the organisation's values; the company talked about a holistic approach, involving ongoing reviews of recruitment and retention policies, how proud they were of their leadership team's commitment and thriving black employee resource group. Yet Nicholas does not feel comfortable there. He is treated like an outsider.

He recalls one example when he was sitting on a MS Teams call and leaning back in his chair whilst he listened. Something his white colleagues did all the time. A private message arrives in the chat:

"You look like you are in a sad RnB video ☹."

Another interviewee shared details about his employer's flagship inclusion initiative to bring in black talent. As a black working-class Oxbridge graduate, the young man earned his place in the firm, yet was asked by a senior colleague, "Oh, did you get into the firm solely because you are on that diversity scheme?" He was proud to be on the scheme, but the tone suggested he had not got his position on merit. This comment would have been less serious had the question not been posed by a colleague who spent a lot of his time promoting that very scheme!

There were mixed responses to some of the training provided to their managers. Three of those I spoke to said that it was a step in the right direction. Another voiced his pragmatic scepticism:

> I'm fully aware that a lot of the people would leave the conversation thinking in their head, "Do you know what? I've had an hour's session learning about microaggression, but I still think these black colleagues are being way too soft, and they need to toughen up and have thicker skin." But they know that to vocalise that in any forum with anyone black is social suicide, and it potentially could hinder their career. Because of that, they will never say such things in a public forum.

THEY UNDERSTAND HOW TO LEVERAGE THEIR BLACKNESS

Two of the young black professionals talked about the value they were able to add to their organisations in helping senior leaders to navigate the language of race and the world of microaggressions. They felt this was an area where they had additional expertise that was valued.

The black men also had an awareness of being perceived as "cool" by their white counterparts. To be confident, intelligent, competent, likeable *and* black was seriously cool. You listen to cool music as perceived by the white, privately educated man or woman. So these white professionals wanted to be in close proximity to you because now you're an interesting person to be around, you have influence – how you carry yourself is interesting. This coolness attracted white male and female colleagues to them. This coolness associated with men was in contrast to the overconfident black female professionals, who still remain in the "aggressive" camp.

The young black professionals noticed that senior white leaders were also keen to be seen to be mentoring them. It had become "fashionable" to have a black mentee. However, they were wary that, for some, this might be a self-promoting, short-term, box-ticking exercise.

NO MORE MODEL BLACK?

Is there space to move away from being the Model Black? With regards to the squaring, self-silencing and softening, I cannot truly know the answer. I am not privy to the conversations of all successful black leaders in organisations. However, this research surfaced very little anti-Model Black behaviour in the business world. It seems that in order to go beyond the Model Black and still be successful, there are three options: the exceptional black, the independent black and the "made it in the organisation already" black.

The exceptional black is the black person who has celebrity cache or is working in certain industries or is considered to be an intellectual genius. These are individuals such as Stormzy or Lewis Hamilton or Afuah Hirsh, the executive team at 0207 Def Jam or the 14-year-old Joshua Beckford, who may occupy positions where they do not need to conform to the Model Black. However, this idea of the exceptional black can be seen as problematic. There is a certain irony because it is the white majority who dictate the spaces in which black people are allowed to thrive, typically sport and music. These are areas where being cool is normative and typically not in organisations. As I mentioned in Chapter 7, Patricia Hill-Collins[6] talks about controlling images in relation to black women, such as the *mammy*. For some, the idea of black exceptionalism, whereby black people are stereotyped into certain roles and industries, could be viewed as a controlling ideology.

The independent black has decided to carve out their own way. In *Black Atlantic*, Gilroy[7] talks about the politics of transfiguration, the idea that black people can use their agency to express themselves outside the existing social order. Those resisting or not wishing to conform to the idea of the Model Black can be viewed as adopting this stance. They set up their own businesses to serve their own communities. These people may have quit the organisation where they were required to act as the Model Black or never joined them because they felt that doing so would require them to surrender a lot of their authenticity.

Finally, there is the "already made it" black who is financially independent or feels that they have gotten to a stage in their career where they are sufficiently established to be who they truly want to be.

VISION FOR THE FUTURE: THE MIDDLE BLACK?

My brother is a career academic. As an expert in black theology, a broadcaster and an author, he has spent his career advocating for black people. He has chosen not to take the path of the Model Black, and I wanted to understand the consequences of making that choice. I also wanted to explore with him future alternatives to the Model Black.

BARBARA: I've inadvertently chosen to be mostly the Model Black. That's what's got me through life. To what extent do you connect with the Model Black?

ROBERT: I would say I've been the complete antithesis because my approach hasn't been the Model Black – it's been more the 'activist' black. Recognising that blackness is always in a struggle, and that means you're always up against it. For me, it means foregrounding blackness first and foremost. Secondly, you are committed to always speaking out. You have also got to be willing to pay the price for being outspoken. This is why I think the activist approach is a narrow path; there are very few activist blacks with a mortgage because you lose your job so many times! Your whole working life is insecure because at some point, you know you're going to have to speak truth to power.

BARBARA: Do you have any regrets for having taken that path?

ROBERT: None.

BARBARA: You've been able to make your way as the 'activist' black in academia. If we are now looking ahead and thinking about black people who are working in a corporate environment, what are the options for them?

ROBERT: Well, I think that there has been a significant and seismic shift in negotiating blackness since the death of George Floyd. I think it's changed everything in the short term, possibly in the long term. Young black people are now saying, my goodness, one can be black, proud, an activist, hold no quarter and be reasonably successful. There's a completely different model of what it means to be black. The second thing is the White Ally Movement, which wasn't there; you had the left and maybe some antiracist groups. Now you've got the White Ally Network within corporations, industries, even within higher education. People who are racialised as white and are prepared to do a lot of the antiracism work. That never really happened before.

These things always have a lifespan, and they depend upon the activist context and things like co-option. We could argue that what we've had is the resistance, the counter-hegemony from the government is the Sewell report, which is a response to the question, "What are we going to do about these activist black people now holding us to account." So we will give them Sewell report which will divide and rule, and we'll say there's no systemic racism!

On the one hand, you've got the Model Black, and on the other hand, you've got the activist black. I think it can be pick-and-mix now. There can be more choices now than the Model Black. You can do the activist black and you can choose when you need to be the activist and when you need to be Model Black, and that's what's happened. There is an alternative now. Consider Beyoncé. When Beyoncé did the Black Power dance at the Super Bowl, people were upset with it. They thought she was white. I think that what Beyoncé did in music can be done in the organisation. You can open up a creative, activist space for black people to have more choice within the workplace; they can play the activist card because it has become much more mainstream to do so.

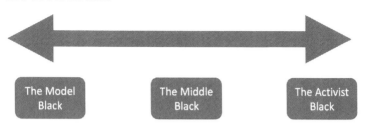

Figure 10.1 The black British leadership spectrum

BARBARA: I like your idea about this mixture between activist and Model Black. Something in the middle. What would the 'middle' black do in the workplace? (See Figure 10.1)

ROBERT: For both the activist black and the Model Black, there is a linguistic component to the politics of transformation. What I mean by that is it's not what you say but how you say it. I think, culturally, we've been at a slight deficit because Caribbean culture is inherently very direct. There's no obfuscation; there's circumlocution. There's no small talk in Jamaica. I'm saying "generally" because not everybody's like that.

In the same way that we ask our white colleagues to learn cultural literacy, there is an activist literacy that black workers have to obtain. I would make that mandatory training. How do you talk to your white colleagues in a way that gets them to do things? That's an art form. Some of us haven't practised that.

African Americans do it really well, particularly in the church context. I've seen really well-educated pastors, Ivy league pastors, like Otis Moss III, from Barack Obama's old church. He's the newly installed pastor, third-generation Ivy league. Brilliant negotiator. Makes everybody feel good. They think, "My goodness, what's the motto of your church?" "Unapologetically black, unashamedly Christian." This linguistic ability to speak truth to power but in a way that is so redemptive and empowering that it doesn't move people away, but it brings them to the table. I think it can be learned in organisations too. It really is about the power of language, and very few people have competency in it. When you do meet them, they are good because they can make black people feel at home, and they are making white people feel at home as well. You know that they haven't sold out.

BARBARA: I love this idea of the power of language. What you have just talked about are the things that black people should or could do. What do you think we need to do to help our white allies or to develop more white allies?

ROBERT: There's something about self-educating, but I think the way to think about it is much more explicit and direct; we need to get them to step out of whiteness. That's what Les Back calls it, the sociologist at Goldsmiths. It means that they understand that the way in which the world is structured means that white men will succeed.

BARBARA: How do we get people to that place of stepping out of whiteness?

ROBERT: I think that what is needed is a conversion experience to blackness. How do we get a white convert? You need to help them understand that there needs to be an ontological shift. It's a psychic conversion to equality. That psychic conversion is more than just knowing. It's about a commitment to radical doing. That can only happen if you have a black conversion experience that feels like really nice. I would say there are very few people racialised as white we know have had it because when they've had it, they've had it. You know that there's a commitment, that something snapped, and they see the world in a different way.

BARBARA: So what happens if you've got these black people, merging the Model Black and the activist black, getting the right vocabulary, and the white people are not undergoing that conversion experience, then what?

ROBERT: It's business as usual, which in Britain means we just repeat the mistakes of the past. The classic example of this is the police force. Twenty-five years after McPherson, there is no significant change in the Metropolitan Police. Why? Because they didn't demand a conversion experience from their management.

BARBARA: So it's about making space for the middle black, and it's about white conversion?

ROBERT: That's right. It should never be a binary position – Model Black or activist, you can do both. You need to be really skilful so that you can take people with you, but you still know who you are and you're comfortable with that. Barack Obama had it. He was so good. He made white people comfortable, made black people comfortable, made white people happy, made black people happy, made black people even think a black person in power could do something for them. I would say Akala does it really, really well; I think that's why people love him. He's clever. Akala went on Piers Morgan, and he just blinded him with statistics. So, the answer is the 'middle' black.

BARBARA: That may be it! The middle, the middle black –

ROBERT: What that means is, the middle black people will be your best allies, more so than the activist or the Model. We need to be looking out for these middle black people who can negotiate these two worlds. Those are the people who really have the best skill set for your company. They can bring the people with them, as well as speaking truth to power.

Not all black people are the same. But what we do know is that there's a deficit of the middle black, and that's why we're struggling. Where's the hope? The hope is that more people occupy this middle black space because it provides a balance between the Model Black and the activist. "The Middle Black" – maybe that's your next book!

KEY TAKEAWAYS

- The Model Black is the *de facto* strategy for the majority of successful black leaders in this study.
- The challenges for young black professionals are very similar to those faced by the black leaders in this research.
- The future of black success in the workplace may be the Middle Black – a fusion of the Model Black and a more "activist" black.

QUESTIONS FOR REFLECTION

- How do you see the future of Inclusion and Diversity in your workplace?
- How are black millennials experiencing your workplace?
- What are your reflections on the concept of the Middle Black?
- What can you do to encourage the emergence of Middle Black in your workplace?

NOTES

1 Pfau, B. N. (2016). What Do Millennials Really Want at Work? The Same Things the Rest of us Do. *Harvard Business Review* 1.

2 Costanza, D. P. et al. (2012). Generational Differences in Work-Related Attitudes: A Meta-Analysis. *Journal of Business and Psychology* 27(4), 375–394.

3 Baird, C. H. (2015). Myths, Exaggerations and Uncomfortable Truths: The Real Story Behind Millennials in the Workplace. *The IBM Institute for Business Value*. www.ibm.com/downloads/cas/Q3ZVGRLP [Last accessed 7 August 2020].

4 Morano-Willams, E. (2020, June 5). Black Lives Matter Activism: The Generational Divide. *Stylus*. www.stylus.com/black-lives-matter-activism-generational-divide [Last accessed November 2021].

5 Business in the Community. *Race at Work Charter*. www.bitc.org.uk/post_tag/race-at-work-charter/ [Last accessed 20 July 2021].

6 Collins, P. H. (2002). *Black Feminist thought: Knowledge, Consciousness, and the Politics of Empowerment*. New York. Routledge.

7 Gilroy, P. (1993). *The Black Atlantic: Modernity and Double Consciousness*. London, New York; Verso.

REFERENCES AND ADDITIONAL READING

Baird, C. H. (2015). Myths, Exaggerations and Uncomfortable Truths: The Real Story Behind Millennials in the Workplace. *The IBM Institute for Business Value*. www.ibm.com/downloads/cas/Q3ZVGRLP [Last accessed 7 August 2020].

Carter, N. M., & Dowe, P. F. (2015). The Racial Exceptionalism of Barack Obama. *Journal of African American Studies* 19(2), 105–119.

Collins, P. H. (1986). Learning from the Outsider Within: The Sociological Significance of Black Feminist thought. *Social Problems* 33(6), s14–s32.

Collins, P. H. (2002). *Black Feminist Thought: Knowledge, Consciousness, and the Politics of Empowerment*. New York. Routledge.

Costanza, D. P. et al. (2012). Generational Differences in Work-Related Attitudes: A Meta-Analysis. *Journal of Business and Psychology* 27(4), 375–394.

Deal, J. J., Altman, D. G., & Rogelberg, S. G. (2010). Millennials at Work: What We Know and What We Need to Do (if Anything). *Journal of Business and Psychology* 25(2), 191–199.

DeVaney, S. A. (2015). Understanding the Millennial Generation. *Journal of Financial Service Professionals* 69(6).

Gilroy, P. (1993). *The Black Atlantic: Modernity and Double Consciousness*. London, New York; Verso.

Morano-Willams, E. (2020, June 5). Black Lives Matter Activism: The Generational Divide. *Stylus*. www.stylus.com/black-lives-matter-activism-generational-divide [Last accessed November 2021].

Ng, E. S., Schweitzer, L., & Lyons, S. T. (2010). New Generation, Great Expectations: A Field Study of the Millennial Generation. *Journal of Business and Psychology* 25(2), 281–292.

Pfau, B. N. (2016). What Do Millennials Really Want at Work? The Same Things the Rest of Us Do. *Harvard Business Review* 1.

TEN THINGS TO CONSIDER NOW THAT YOU HAVE READ THIS BOOK

Black leaders have shown honesty and openness as they have shared their stories. My hope is that the experiences contained within this book have opened your mind and your organisation's understanding of what it takes to be a black leader in 21st-century Britain. Every employee, manager and leader will have an opinion on what comes next. For quick action, I suggest the following ten questions to make progress straight away. Please feel free to add your own or contact the DEI leader in your organisation.

- To what extent has the book altered your understanding of the black British leadership experience?
- What, if any, was your emotional response to reading this book?
- How similar or different were the Model Black leadership experiences to those of your own?
- How can you use your learning from this book to lead in a way that allows all under-represented groups to contribute to their fullest?
- What can you do to continue your education in the area of inclusive leadership more generally?
- How can you influence the Equity, Diversity and Inclusion agenda in your organisation?
- What one thing can you do tomorrow to increase Equity, Diversity and Inclusion in your workplace?
- How might reading this book impact the relationships you have with colleagues who are different from yourself?
- What can you do to allow space for the development of the Middle Black?
- How comfortable do you *now* feel about having a conversation around race?

DOI: 10.4324/9781003200482-16

INDEX

Page numbers in *italics* indicate a figure on the corresponding page.